NAZI GERMANY
A HISTORY OF THE THIRD REICH

A new and comprehensive study of the events that enabled

Adolf Hitler and Nazi Germany to change the course of History

David Anversa

2020 © David Anversa

All rights are reserved

Contents:

Chapter one 5
Introduction: What influenced the events 5
Nazi Party Origins 8
Hyperinflation and the Fallout 13
Chapter two 21
What motivated Adolf Hitler? 21
Brew Hall Putsch 23
Writing his biography 23
Aryan Race: 24
The Schutzstaffel (SS) 26
Sources of the SS 27
Heinrich Himmler, Architect of the SS 28
Eva Braun 29
Chapter three 34
Early years of being 34
Chapter four 54
Trade and Commerce 54
Chapter five 73
The Jewish Question 73
What was Auschwitz? 81
How did Auschwitz work? 82
The Last Solution 83
Key Dates 84

Chapter Six 89

Second World War 89

Germany victories (1939/1942) 93

> Germany did not defeat Great Britain, which was shielded from German assault by the English Channel, Royal Navy and Royal Air Force (Raf) 93

An altered record of the meeting follows 103

1. Trials managing the endurance of military staff 105
2. Analyses to test medications and medicines 105
3. Analyses to propel Nazi racial and philosophical objectives: 106

The Nuremberg Code 108

Chapter Seven 109

The events that followed? 109

Ascending the stepping stool 112

Chapter Eight 118

Conclusion 118

Key Dates 119

Chapter one

Introduction: What influenced the events

It was early in the year of 1933 when the tension in Berlin rose, pronouncing the end of the country of Weimar. Twenty-eight days into the New Year, on January 28, General Kurt Von Schleicher – the chancellor of the state - after 57 days in office, was dismissed by the Field Marshal Von Hindenburg. This unfortunate winter weekend is remembered in History to decide Germany's fate for nearly a century to come.

Adolf Hitler, the chairman of the Nationalist Socialist Party, had religiously for two years before put forward his name to be elected as the chancellor, and was repeatedly turned down. While the Weimar republic since its formation had been a success, nearly 13 years later, in January of the New Year, there were talks of *Putsch* (German for Coup) by one party and its many generals.

Adolf Hitler had always dreamed of making Germany-Austria one – under the German Flag, and all his efforts were to ensure that. Little did everyone know this idea borne into the head of a madman was a solemn vow to destroy all of Germany?

Dr. Joseph Goebbels, as acclaimed by David Irving in this

book as the mastermind of the Third Reich, in his biography, wrote that Monday, June 30, was a solemn day for them. Hitler - their leader, went into the chancellery to determine the country's future; along with many other Nazi generals, he stood outside the gates of Kaiserhof, waiting to see their leader's expression. They had the notion in their minds that would be able to tell if they had won or not, by his expression. He was confident they would be able to read his face, for they had stood outside these gates, seldom times for a few years – it was a sense of déjà vu, to anticipate joy or failure, or mere astonishment, were they ever successful.

All they wanted was a miracle, and they stood there – witnessing it firsthand.

Who was Adolf Hitler? A sickly boy born in the forgotten town of Braunau-on-the-Inn. This town itself was directly half-and-half between Austria and Germany, *to unite which was the dream of almost every child born in that area*, or the very least devote their life to the mission of; as he did – even in times of being a low-life no one knew about in Vienna.

Before getting into the events that happened, it is first essential to understand how he came to be, following into the Third Reich series of events.

The Nazi Party developed into a mass development and controlled Germany through extremist methods from 1933 to 1945 under the initiative of Adolf Hitler (1889-

1945). Established in 1919 as the German Workers' Party, the gathering advanced German pride and was hostile to Semitism and communicated disappointment with the Treaty of Versailles' details. This 1919 harmony settlement finished World War I (1914-1918) and expected Germany to make various concessions and reparations. Hitler joined the gathering the year it was established and turned into its pioneer in 1921. The year 1933, he became chancellor of Germany, and his government before long was running in tyrannical forces. After Germany's annihilation in World War II (1939-45), the Nazi Party saw its most anticipated end. Many
of its high-ranking representatives received life sentences for atrocities identified with the murder of somewhere in the range of 6 million European Jews during the Holocaust.

Nazi Party Origins

In 1919, armed forces veteran Adolf Hitler, baffled by Germany's thrashing in World War I, left the country. He was financially discouraged and politically insecure but joined a political association called the German Workers' Party. Established that same year by a little gathering of men including locksmith Anton Drexler (1884-1942) and writer Karl Harrer (1890-1926), the gathering advanced German patriotism and stood against Semitism. The core ideas were that the Treaty of Versailles, the harmony settlement that finished the war, was incredibly harmful to Germany by mandating reparations it would never pay. Before long, Hitler tapped into being a magnetic public speaker and started reaching new members with talks of accusing Jews and Marxists of Germany's issues and embracing outrageous patriotism with the idea of an Aryan "ace race." In July 1921, he accepted the association's authority, renamed the Nationalist Socialist German Workers' (Nazi) Party.

Altogether his reign was bloody and annihilating. However, even more gruesome were the events that led to his position as the future Fuehrer.

It was the start of the late 18th century after the United States had announced its independence from Great Britain. Central Europe was then an accumulation of 300 or more states.

In the early 19th century, Germany had approximately 39 states, all of which had somewhat similar political interests. Under the German Confederation's name in 1815, these states came together to unite all German-speaking states' economies. While there are many who think had this idea been a success, Germany today would have flourished and have held more power over the world than it already does, but in the time of its being, the German Confederation stood against everything which a pure German Nationalist at heart stands for.

Before it could indeed be proven, it collapsed within a few years due to the ever-increasing enmity of the two powerful states of Austria and Prussia. Many talks, falling out, and a seven years' war later, Germany came to be known as the German Empire, or, in other words, the start of the first German Reich, led by its first chancellor Otto Von Bismarck.

In many ways, Adolf Hitler and Otto Bismarck are the same. Unfortunately, the two nationalists at heart could never meet. The former was nine years old when the latter died. Nevertheless, many, including Adolf Hitler's close friends, believed that he, in his twisted way, admired the goal Bismarck had for a united Germany, even though he had failed to bring Austria under its flag.

The first Reich or Germany's unification had brought all German states under its flag except Austria. There are many speculations to why it happened, and Adolf Hitler, in his own opinion, thought of it as an agenda to neglect Austria, for his biggest weakness was his love for Austria and Germany together.

It was a widely known fact that Austria and Prussia had no love for each other, and when the talks for Unified Germany began, Austria itself did not want to be part of it. Austria had a dual monarchy, which it would have to give up to be a part of unified Germany – a Prussia dominated Germany – for this reason, King Habsburg, ruler of the Holy Roman Empire, neglected it.

Otto Von Bismarck led the first German Reich in 1871 by the exclusion of Austria.

Nonetheless, this led to the spark of German nationalism, which later was led by many prominent leaders and dictators, and which has consumed the German people.

Otto Von Bismarck was an expert in the fields of politics and the military. He ruled the newly formed German Empire with an iron grip. Like Hitler, he was cunning and had the knack for manipulating people to his will. Above all, what they had in common was their love for Germany. A unified Nation, which flourished, and, in their dream, ruled over all of Europe. He was the greatest Prussian politician Germany had seen in its history.

Paul Von Hindenburg and Erich Ludendorff led unified Germany through World War I, which proved to be a difficult task for they neither had the same dreams nor the manifestation to hold the reins. They tried their best to lead the country through the draughts of a War that was one of its kind. November that same year sparked yet another revolution, abolishing monarchism in all of Europe, giving birth to Nazism, a concept and power to a soldier who had fought and survived in Vienna – Adolf Hitler.

The backbone of Nazi Germany will always be the Weimar Republic, or later in Hitler's words, will be known as the Second Reich. Germany took a turn from being a federation run by a monarch and royal families to democracy until the Nazi uprising in 1933 marked its end.

The Weimar Republic was Germany's legislature from 1919 to 1933, the period after World War I until Hitler's reign began. The constitution was shaped by a public get together after Kaiser Wilhelm II surrendered. From its unsure beginnings to a short period of accomplishment and a feeling of overwhelming sorrow, the Weimar Republic experienced turmoil to situate Germany for the ascent of Adolf Hitler and the Nazi Party.

The Weimar Constitution was signed into law by President Ebert on August 11, 1919. The law confronted venomous resistance from the military and the extreme left. The constitution contained 181 articles and secured everything from the German state (Reich) and the German individuals' privileges to strict opportunity and how laws ought to be authorized.

The Weimar Constitution incorporated these features:

- The Chancellor or a Reich Minister must support all acts of the President.
- Article 48 permits the President to suspend social liberties and work freely in a crisis.
- Two authoritative bodies (the Reichstag and the Reichsrat) were to speak for the German public.
- All Germans have similar social liberties and duties.
- All Germans reserve the privilege to the opportunity of articulation.
- All Germans reserve the privilege to tranquil get together.
- All Germans reserve the privilege of the opportunity of religion; there is no state church.
- State-run, government-funded instruction is free and compulsory for youngsters.
- All Germans have the privilege of private property.
- All Germans reserve the option to approach opportunity and income in the work environment.

Hyperinflation and the Fallout

Regardless of its new constitution, the Weimar Republic confronted one of Germany's most prominent monetary difficulties: hyperinflation. On account of the Treaty of Versailles, Germany's capacity to deliver income-producing coal and iron mineral diminished. As war obligations and reparations depleted its coffers, the German government could not pay its obligations.

A portion of the previous World War I Allies did not accept Germany's case that it could not bear to pay. In an obtrusive League of Nations penetrate, French and Belgian soldiers involved Germany's fundamental industrial zone, the Ruhr Valley, resolved to get their reparation installments.

The Weimar government requested German specialists to actively oppose the occupation and picket, closing down the coal mineshafts and iron processing plants. Thus, Germany's economy immediately failed.

Accordingly, the Weimar government essentially printed more cash. The exertion exploded backward, and further degraded the German mark—and inflation grew at an astonishing level. The average cost for essential items rose quickly, and numerous individuals lost all they had.

During hyperinflation, the German working class endured the worst part of the financial disarray. Within a few years, the people soon were tired and doubtful of their leaders. Looking for a new initiative and dreading a Communist takeover, numerous individuals went to radical gatherings, for example, the Nazi Party led by Adolf Hitler, notwithstanding his disagreeable and bombed endeavor to begin a public insurgency in 1923.

In 1932, the Nazi Party turned into the biggest party in Parliament. After a brief battle for power, Hitler was named Chancellor in January 1933. In a few weeks, he used Article 48 of the Weimar Constitution to subdue numerous social equality groups and stifle individuals from the Communist faction.

In March 1933, Hitler used the Enabling Act, permitting him to pass laws without the endorsement of Germany's Parliament or President. Because Hitler wanted this act passed at any cost, he persuasively kept Communist Parliament members from casting a ballot. When it became law, Hitler was allowed to rule as he saw fit and set up his autocracy with no balanced governance.

Blaming Germany's problems on Jews, backstabbers, socialists, and the disappointments of the Weimar majority rules system, Hitler and Hindenburg stood against each other in the 1932 presidential elections. Hindenburg won, yet Hitler got 37 percent of the vote. In July, 14 million Germans decided in favor of the Nazis in new parliamentary races, making Hitler's gathering the biggest in the Reichstag with 37 percent of the seats.

Proceeding with political disturbance came about in one more Reichstag political decision scarcely four months later. The Nazis lost a few seats in the Reichstag; however, the Communist Party picked up seats, which drove a broad scope of gatherings to back Hitler.

At long last, on January 30, 1933, President Hindenburg hesitantly consented to pick Hitler as the new Chancellor. Hitler vowed to watch the Weimar Constitution and structure a comprehensive alliance government to unravel the financial emergency.

The government officials exhorting Hindenburg told him they could control the upstart from Bavaria. One political pioneer stated, "In two months we will have driven Hitler into a corner so hard he will be squeaking."

Hitler, in any case, immediately outmaneuvered different lawmakers. He convinced Hindenburg to call another political election while administering by decree. One order limited ideological group meetings and the press.

During the political race, part of the Reichstag burned to the ground. Hitler accused the socialists. He gave another "brief" order, suspending sacred rights to squash the socialists.

In March 1933, with near 6 million Germans jobless, the Nazi Party won 44 percent of the Reichstag seats. With the help of smaller traditional parties, Hitler instructed the lion's share to shape another parliament.

Hitler presented an "Empowering Act," requiring the Reichstag to move its lawmaking forces to him. The law additionally permitted Hitler to overlook any arrangement of the previous government.

On March 23, 1933, the national assembly met in a Berlin drama house to decide on the Enabling Act. With the walkways filled with Nazi tempest troopers, the Reichstag cast a ballot to end popular government in Germany and make Hitler tyrant of what he called the "Third Reich."

It is altogether hard to envision a more impossible figure to prevail to Bismarck's mantle, the Hohenzollern sovereigns, and President Hindenburg than this solitary Austrian worker.

The place of birth on the Austro-German outskirts was to demonstrate noteworthy, for, as a simple youth, Hitler got fixated on the possibility that there should be no fringe between these two German-speaking groups and that both had a place in a similar Reich. So reliable and suffering were his sentiments that at 35 when he sat in a German jail directing the book that would turn into the outline for the Third Reich, his first lines were worried about the emblematic importance of his origin.

The evening of Nov. 9-10, 1938 — known as Kristallnacht, the evening of broken glass — temples were set to fire, stores wholly destroyed, and Jewish homes turned into urban areas and towns all over the Third Reich. Firemen and police held on, trained possibly to mediate if neighboring "Aryan" property resisted. Over the next days, many Jews were captured and detained in nearby correctional facilities, improvised penitentiaries, and around 30,000 sent to death camps. Hundreds of families disported, lives laid to waste, livestock lost, handfuls ended it all. Germans and Austrians of Jewish ancestry had no future in their own country. Some figured out how to emigrate, forsaking property and loved ones; those abandoned would later be sent to the killing camps in the east.

Describing it like this, in the passive voice, features the brutality that went against Jews. What is more, at this commemoration of such a sad occasion, it is correct that we recall the people in question. However, who was dependable? What exercises would we be able to adapt today, in the wake of the deadly assault on Jews in the Pittsburgh Tree of Life place of worship?

The fear was inflicted on the above, endorsed by Hitler and released by Goebbels. The significant culprits were the undeniable Nazis — the dark booted SS, the earthy colored shirted SA, the optimistic Hitler Youth, the individuals from the subsidiary associations gladly displaying insignias and gathering identifications.

However, the more extensive populace's reactions also made it conceivable — and this is the thing that must at present give us cause for thought today.

Enormous quantities of conventional individuals, including

ladies, were associated with plundering and ravaging, selecting up products tossed onto the road, and profiting by Jewish property's confiscation. Both young and old ended up humiliating Jews, with entire classes of schoolchildren brought by their educators to see locales of seething worship places and join the steering groups. While some were egged on by peer pressure, numerous youngsters accepted the Nazi view that the *"Jews are our incident" and that it was "an ideal opportunity to take care of them."*

In any case, some stated that they were "embarrassed to be German," and were reproachful of the brutality against individuals and the obliteration of property. Such remarks are accounted for in numerous contemporary sources and onlooker accounts from all over the Reich.

However, for what reason did many not rise to dissent? For what reason did observers remain, to a great extent, quiet, inactive?

For starters, there is the conspicuous point about state-appointed dread. The brutality started early, in a state where the dynamic political restrictions were no more, where it is amazingly hard to take part in powerful obstruction. Numerous political activists had just emigrated, regularly after early spells in death camps, some looking to battle on from abroad. Following a time of constraint, many of the residents had no choice but to follow into silence. In November 1938, however, a few people figured out how to give secret help, many who dreaded severe punishments remained uninvolved, whatever their compassion toward the abused.

With such underlying circumstances, there is yet another more perplexing point concerning the longer-term consistency with a predominant atmosphere of aggression toward those authoritatively slandered as the "other."

By 1938, with Hitler in power for more than five years, most non-Jewish Germans had obliged to live under the Nazi system. Huge numbers were excited allies of Hitler and his declared re-visitation of public enormity; many more joined the Nazi party (NSDAP) or subsidiary associations for entrepreneurial reasons. Others bargained less eagerly, performing new roles in broad daylight and murmuring differences secretly, however fearful of being condemned if they stepped out of line.

Whether through longstanding or recently procured conviction or constrained congruity, individuals rejected Jews from their public activities, their friendship circles, and their recreation affiliations, and lost contact with Jews who had been tossed out of their jobs and compelled to abandon their homes. With expanding social and physical partition between networks, "Aryans" — individuals from Hitler's misleading "ace race" — lost contact with the prohibited "non-Aryans." Furthermore, with developing obliviousness of their breaking down circumstance came a scholarly lack of concern to their destiny.

This sneaking consistency, in actuality, added up to complicity.

Set forth plainly: the Nazi administration had presented a threatening situation and started viable measures, regardless of whether through enactment or savagery, to set up an ethnically characterized "individuals' locale."

By being generally agreeable, for whatever reasons, those who were not prohibited had assisted with making a considerably more cold condition – one in which it was possible to dread visibly to everyone without significant distress or mediation for the abused.

The assignment "Third Reich" was initiated in 1922 by the sentimental moderate, völkisch-patriot scholarly essayist Arthur Moeller van cave Bruck. In his distribution Das Dritte Reich (The Third Reich), Moeller imagined the ascent of an enemy of liberalism, hostile to the Marxist Germanic Empire in which all social class divisions were to take into account the public solidarity under a magnetic "Führer" (pioneer). Moeller's "Third Reich" alluded to two past Germanic Empires: Charlemagne's middle age Frankish Empire and the German Empire under the Prussian Hohenzollern administration (1871-1918).

Chapter two

What motivated Adolf Hitler?

He was born in a little Austrian town close to the Austro-German border. Alois, Adolf Hitler's father, worked as a state customs official all his life, while his son spent most of his adolescence in Linz, the capital of Upper Austria.

Not having any desire to emulate his dad's profession as a government employee, he started battling in optional school and, in the end, dropped out. Alois died in 1903, and Adolf sought his fantasy about being an artist; however, he was soon afterward expelled from Vienna's Academy of Fine Arts.

After his mother, Klara, died in 1908, Hitler moved to Vienna, where he sorted out a living painting landscapes and landmarks and selling the pictures. Forlorn and secluded, Hitler got inspired by legislative issues during his years in Vienna and created a most of the thoughts that would shape the Nazi belief system.

In 1913, Hitler moved to Munich in the German territory of Bavaria. When World War I broke out the next summer, he requested the Bavarian lord to be permitted to chip in a save infantry regiment.

Conveyed in October 1914 to Belgium, Hitler served all through the Great War and won two medals for valor including the uncommon Iron Cross First Class, which he wore to the end of his life.

Hitler was injured twice during the war. He was shot in the leg at Somme in 1916 and incidentally blinded by a British gas assault close to Ypres in 1918. After a month, he was recovering in a medical clinic at Pasewalk, northeast of Berlin, when the news showed up of the truce and Germany's destruction in World War I.

In the same way as other Germans, Hitler came to accept the nation's overwhelming destruction could be credited not to the Allies, but to inadequately devoted "deceivers" at home—a legend that would sabotage the post-war Weimar Republic and set up Hitler's ascent.

After Hitler got back to Munich in late 1918, he joined the little German Workers' Party, which intended to join the interests of the common laborers with a solid German patriotism.

In one of Hitler's virtuoso strokes, the recently renamed National Socialist German Workers Party, or Nazi Party, embraced a variant of the Hakenkreuz's antiquated image snared cross, as its symbol. Imprinted in a white hover is Hitler's insignia would take on the unnerving representative force in the years to come.

Before the end of 1921, Hitler led the developing Nazi Party, profiting by inevitable disagreements with the Weimar Government and by constantly rebuffing terms of the Versailles Treaty. Many disappointed previous military officials in Munich would join the Nazis, like Ernst Rohm, who selected the "solid arm" crews—known as the Sturmabteilung (SA)— which Hitler used to secure gatherings and assault rivals.

Brew Hall Putsch

On the night of November 8, 1923, individuals from the SA and others pushed their way into a vast brew hall where another conservative head was tending to the group. Using a gun, Hitler announced the start of public unrest and drove marchers to the center of Munich, where they got into a fight with police. Hitler fled but was later captured, along with his other renegade pioneers. Although it bombed breathtakingly, the Beer Hall Putsch built up Hitler as a public figure.

Writing his biography

In 1924, charged with treason against his nation, Hitler's sentence was five years in jail. However, he was out in nine months from the general solace of Landsberg Castle. During this period, he started to write the book that would become "Mein Kampf" ("My Struggle").

In it, Hitler developed the nationalistic, anti-Semitic

perspectives he had started to create in Vienna in his mid-twenties, and spread out designs for Germany—and the world—he tried to make when he took control.

Hitler would complete the second volume of "Mein Kampf" after his release while unwinding in Berchtesgaden's mountain air. It sold unobtrusively from the start, yet it turned into Germany's top of the line book after the Bible with Hitler's ascent. By 1940, it had sold around 6 million copies there.

Hitler's subsequent book, "The Zweites Buch," was written in 1928 and contained his international strategy plans. However, for the helpless beginning deals of "Mein Kampf", it was distributed after his death. The primary English translations of "The Zweites Buch" did not show up until 1962 and was distributed under the title "Hitler's Secret Book."

Aryan Race:

Fixated on race and the possibility of ethnic "virtue," Hitler saw a characteristic plan that put the alleged "Aryan race" at the top.

For him, the Volk (the German public) would locate its most genuine manifestation not in fair or parliamentary Government, but in one incomparable pioneer, or Führer.

"Mein Kampf" likewise tended to the requirement for

Lebensraum (or living space): To satisfy its predetermination, Germany should assume control over grounds toward the east that were currently inhabited by "substandard" Slavic groups—including Austria, the Sudetenland (Czechoslovakia), Poland and Russia.

The Schutzstaffel (SS)

When Hitler left jail, financial assistance had reestablished some well-known help for the Weimar Republic, and backing for traditional causes like Nazism had all the earmarks of melting away.

Throughout the following years, Hitler disappeared and tried to redesign and reshape the Nazi Party. He built up the Hitler Youth to sort out adolescents and made the Schutzstaffel (SS) a more reliable option than the SA.

Individuals from the SS wore dark garb and swore an individual promise of unwaveringness to Hitler. (After 1929, under the initiative of Heinrich Himmler, the SS would create from a gathering of somewhere in the range of 200 men a power that would overwhelm Germany and threaten the remainder of involved Europe during World War II.)

Established in 1925, the "Schutzstaffel," German for "Defensive Echelon," at first filled in as Nazi Party pioneer Adolf Hitler's (1889-1945) individual protectors, and later got one of the most impressive and dreaded associations in all of Nazi Germany. Heinrich Himmler (1900-45), an intense enemy of Semites, like Hitler, became top of the Schutzstaffel, or SS, in 1929 and extended the its job and size. By the beginning of World War II (1939-45), the SS had more than 250,000 members and various developments, occupied with exercises extending from knowledge tasks to running Nazi death camps. At the after war Nuremberg trials, the SS was regarded as a criminal association for its immediate contribution to atrocities.

Sources of the SS

In 1921, Adolf Hitler became the pioneer of a young political association called the National Socialist German Workers' (Nazi) Party. The gathering advanced outrageous German patriotism and hostility to Semitism and was disappointed with the Treaty of Versailles, the 1919 harmony settlement that finished World War I (1914-18) and required various concessions reparations from Germany. Hitler accused Jews and Marxists of Germany's problems and upheld the idea of an Aryan "ace race."

Before the end of 1921, Hitler had his private armed force, the "Sturmabteilung" ("Assault Division"), or SA, whose individuals were known as tempest troopers or earthy colored shirts (for the shade of their garb). The SA went with Hitler during his public appearances and encompassed him when he gave ardent discourses encouraging his allies to execute viciousness against Jews and his political foes.

In 1925, Hitler requested the arrangement of the Schutzstaffel, an element that was discrete from, albeit connected to, the SA. The SS at first comprised of eight people, every one of whom were dependent on monitoring Hitler and other top Nazis. Julius Schreck (1898-1936), a devoted Hitler follower, turned into the SS's prominent leader. The next year, Schreck, who as often as possible wore a fake mustache that took after Hitler's, was supplanted by Joseph Berchtold (1897-1962). Erhard Heiden (1901-33) assumed responsibility for the SS in 1927. That same year, SS individuals were told not to participate in political discussion and were needed to pronounce undying unwaveringness to Hitler and unquestioningly recognize him as their unrivaled prophet.

Heinrich Himmler, Architect of the SS

On January 6, 1929, Hitler named Heinrich Himmler officer of the SS, which had nearly 300 individuals. Himmler, who, like Hitler, was an intense enemy of Semites, hosted combined the Nazi Get in 1923 and, in the end, filled in as Hitler's purposeful publicity boss. Himmler resolved to isolate the SS from the SA, change the SS into a world-class power that was bigger and more intense than the SA, and, at long last, modify the association's capacity inside the Nazi Party.

Under Himmler's direction, the SS developed throughout the following four years into a top-notch paramilitary unit. To fit the SS's bill, imminent individuals needed to demonstrate that none of their predecessors were Jewish and consent to wed distinctly with their boss officials' assent. The military training sessions were so intense as if they were the tip-top of the Nazi Party. Regardless of anything else, they were to esteem devotion and commitment to the Nazi ideal, place particular concerns aside, and play out their obligations tirelessly and as a durable unit. Such desires were reflected in the SS saying: "Unwaveringness is my honor."

Eva Braun

Hitler spent a significant part of his life at Berchtesgaden during these years, and his stepsister, Angela Raubal, and her two little girls frequently went along with him. After Hitler got charmed by his delightful blonde niece, Geli Raubal, his possessive desire drove her to commit suicide in 1931.

Crushed by the misfortune, Hitler would consider Geli the principal genuine romantic undertaking of his life. Before long, he started an involved acquaintance with Eva Braun, a right shop hand from Munich, yet would not wed her.

The Great Depression that started in 1929 again compromised the solidness of the Weimar Republic. Resolved to use political force to influence his insurgency, Hitler developed Nazi help among German preservationists, including armed forces, business, and modern pioneers.

Hitler did not start the disdain of Jews. Jews in Europe had been survivors of separation and mistreatment since the

Middle Ages, regularly for strict reasons. Christians considered being confident as a deviation. Jews, however, had to change over, or they were not permitted to work in certain professions. In the nineteenth century, religion assumed a less significant role. It was made clear by the speculations about the contrasts among races and people groups. The possibility that Jews had a place with unexpected people compared to the Germans, for example, got on. Indeed, even Jews who had changed over to Christianity were still 'unique' due to their bloodline.

The cause of Hitler's contempt for Jews is not exact. In Mein Kampf, he portrayed his advancement into bigotry due to a long, individual battle. As far as anyone knows, his abhorrence for everything Jewish happened as expected when he was living and functioning as a painter in Vienna (1908-1913). Most antiquarians accept that Hitler thought of this clarification looking back. He would have utilized it to guarantee individuals who differed from his light psychology in the long run. One way or another, Hitler came into contact with bigoted thoughts at an early age. How much he shared them by then, is not sure. If he was biased against Jews while living in Vienna, his preference had not yet solidified into an unmistakable perspective. One of the most faithful purchasers of his artistic creations in Vienna was a Jew, Samuel Morgenstern.

The concrete evidence suggests that two Austrian government officials extraordinarily affected Hitler's reasoning. The first, Georg Ritter von Schönerer (1842-

1921), was a German patriot. He accepted that the German-talking districts of Austria-Hungary had to be under the German domain. He additionally felt that Jews would never be entirely German citizens. From the second, the Viennese civic chairman Karl Lueger (1844-1910), Hitler figured out how discrimination against Jews and social changes could be fruitful. In Mein Kampf, Hitler adulated Lueger as 'the best German civic chairman of all times.' When Hitler came to power in 1933, he set up comparable thoughts as a regular occurrence.

The First World War assumed a definitive part in Hitler's life. It gave his life, which had been somewhat fruitless up to that point, a reason. In 1914, he enrolled in the German armed forces, which was battling France, England, and Russia, along with the Austro-Hungarian Empire. Even though he saw little activity, he got an honor for fortitude shown. When Germany surrendered in November 1918, Hitler was in a military emergency clinic. He had eye injuries by a toxin gas assault in Belgium. Kept to his sickbed, he heard the German acquiescence updates, which drove him into a profound emergency. He wrote that 'all that started to go dark again before my eyes.' Stumbling, he grabbed his way back to the quarters and burrowed his consuming head in cover and pillow.

The German thrashing was challenging to accept for some Germans, and Hitler, as well. In patriot and traditional moderate circles, the 'betray legend' became mainstream. As indicated by this fantasy, Germany did not lose the war on the war zone, but through treachery at the home front.

The Jews, Social Democrats, and Communists were held responsible. The partialities about the function of the Jews in the war were bogus. An examination done by the German Government demonstrated such a lot. More than 100,000 German and Austrian Jews had battled for their fatherland. Otto Frank, who had faced the Somme's Conflict in 1916, was only one of them.

Against the background of transformation and viciousness, Hitler's discrimination against Jews was getting progressively extremist. He had seldom stated that he did not uphold uncontrolled 'passionate' massacres (upheavals of against Jewish savagery). Instead, he contended for a 'discrimination against Jews of the mind.' It must be lawful and would eventually prompt the 'expulsion' of the Jews. As right on time as of August 1920, Hitler contrasted the Jews with germs. He expressed that infections were impossible to control, except by obliterating their causes. The Jews' impact could never vanish without eliminating its motivation, the Jew, from our middle, he said. These extreme thoughts were made ready for the mass homicide of the Jews during the 1940s.

Hitler reprimanded the Jews for all that was not right with the world. Germany was powerless and in decay due to the 'Jewish impact.' As indicated by Hitler, the Jews were after world dominance. What is more, they would not spare a moment to utilize every single imaginable mean, including free enterprise. Along these lines, Hitler exploited the current partiality that connected the Jews to money related influence and monetary gain. Hitler was not annoyed by the apparent logical inconsistencies in his reasoning. He held that socialism was Jewish connivance, as the more prominent aspect of the socialist chiefs was Jewish - that to some extent, the Jews were socialists. This thought of 'Jewish socialism' was to have dreadful repercussions in the war with the Soviet Union that began in 1941. The populace and detainees of war were dealt with severely by the Germans.

Hitler saw the world as a field for the perpetual battle between peoples. He isolated the total populace into high and low races. The Germans had a place with the high people groups and the Jews with the low ones. He additionally had detailed thoughts about different groups. The Slavic public, for example, was given a role as substandard, foreordained to be dominated. Hitler felt that the German public must be stable if they were 'unadulterated.' As a result, individuals with genetic sicknesses were unsafe.

These included individuals with physical or mental inabilities, just as drunkards and 'hopeless' lawbreakers. When the Nazis had come to control, these thoughts prompted the constrained disinfection and slaughtering of people.

Chapter three

Early years of being

The hypothesis which Hitler had developed in his drifter days in Vienna and never overlooked – that the best approach to control for a progressive development was to align itself with a portion of the fantastic organizations in the State – had now turned out to be in practice basically as he had determined. The President, supported by the Army, and the traditionalists, had made him Chancellor. His political force, however incredible, was, in any case, not complete. It imparted to these three wellsprings of authority, which had placed him into the office and outside and, to a few degrees, incredulous of the National Socialist development.

Hence, Hitler's prompt assignment was to dispense with them from the driver's seat rapidly, make his group the selective ace of the State, and afterward, with the intensity of a tyrant government and its police, complete the Nazi unrest. He had been in office barely 24 hours when he made his first unequivocal move, unveiling a snare to his guileless moderate "captors" and setting in motion a chain of occasions which he either started or controlled and which toward the finish of a half year would bring the total Nazification of Germany. Furthermore, his rise to the Reich's despot bound together and defederalized for the first time in German history.

Five hours after being confirmed, in 1933, Hitler held his first bureau meeting. The minutes of the meeting, which turned up at Nuremberg among the many vast amounts of caught mystery records, uncover how rapidly and adeptly Hitler, helped by the sly Goering, started to take his moderate partners for a ride. Hindenburg had named Hitler to head, not a presidential bureau but dependent on the majority in the Reichstag. Nonetheless, the Nazis and the Nationalists, the main two gatherings spoke to in the legislature, had just 247 seats out of 583 in Parliament and, in this manner, did not have the majority. To achieve it, they required the support of the Center Party with its 70 seats. In the first hours of the new Government, Hitler had dispatched Goering to talk with the Centrist heads, and now he answered to the bureau that the Center was requesting "certain concessions."

Hugenberg, a wooden brain man for all his accomplishments, protested, taking the focus into the legislature. However, new decisions concerning Nazis with State's assets behind them may win a flat out dominant part at the surveys. They may also be in a situation to administer with his administrations and those of his moderate companions. He proposed practically smothering the Communist Party; with its 100 seats wiped out, the Nazis and the Nationalists would have a larger part. Hitler would not go so far at that moment, and it was, at last, concurred that he would meet with the Center Party pioneers the next morning and that if the discussions were pointless, the bureau would then request new races.

Hitler effortlessly made them unprofitable. At his solicitation, the Center chief, Monsignor Kaas, submitted as a reason for conversation a rundown of inquiries which included an interest that Hitler guarantee to administer intrinsically. Nevertheless, Hitler, deceiving both Kaas and his bureau individuals, answered to the last that the Center had set outlandish expectations and that there was zero chance of agreement. He accordingly recommended that the President dissolve the Reichstag and call new elections. Both Hugenberg and Papen had gotten caught, yet after a profound affirmation from the Nazi chief that the bureau would stay unaltered however the races turned out, they consented to oblige him. The date of the new race was March 5.

In the last generally free political race, Germany was to have the Nazi Party utilize all the administration's enormous assets to win votes. Goebbels was glad. "Presently, it will be simple," he wrote in his journal on February 3, "to carry on the battle, for we can approach all the assets of the State. Radio and press are available to us. We will arrange a magnum opus of purposeful publicity. What is more, this time, normally, there is no absence of money."

The colossal money managers, satisfied with the new Government that planned to put the sorted out laborers in their place and leave the board to maintain its organizations as it wished, were approached to pay up. They agreed at a gathering on February 20 at Goering's Reichstag President's Palace. There, Dr. Schacht went about as host, and Goering and Hitler set out the line to a few dozen of Germany's driving magnates, including Krupp von Bohlen, who had gotten an excited Nazi short-term, Bosch and Schnitzler of I. G. Farben, and Voegler, top of the United Steel Works.

Hitler started a long discourse with a sop to the industrialists. *"Private undertaking,"* he stated, "cannot be kept up in the time of popular government; *it is possible just if the individuals have a sound thought of power and character . . . All the common merchandise we have we owe to the battle of the picked . . . We should not disregard that all the advantages of culture must be presented pretty much with an iron clench hand."*

He guaranteed the money managers that he would "dispense with" the Marxists; what is more, reestablish the Wehrmacht (the last was of uncommon enthusiasm to such enterprises).

During the Great Depression, paper inclusion was the principal wellspring of data about global political occasions, and papers were necessary during the time spent assembling, conveying, and introducing data to general society. Not only did the paper convey the news, it also moved a general mentality and scrutinized the news it introduced, dependent on its style, word decision, and introduction, and shed light on how global news brought change to the American public. The announcing of Hitler's ascent to control in Germany and the severe developing strategies of the early Nazi system are a specific way to perceive how a chronicled improvement we would see as inauspicious today with carelessness endorsement just irregular worry from paper distributors at that point. This paper will review Adolf Hitler and the Nazi Party in Germany from issues of The Seattle Times, one of the city's important newspapers, in 1933. As Hitler rose to control, The Seattle Times was at first reluctant to investigate the Nazi Party, and printed numerous articles consoling readers of his tranquil points, even while writing about the enemy of Jewish suppression. Toward the year's end, would The Times become worried about Hitler's developing force, a pattern that reveals insight into the Government's appearing absence of worry about Nazi suppression in the early long periods of Hitler's system?

In January of 1933, Adolf Hitler turned into a conspicuous world figure as the pioneer of Germany and the Nazi party. The Seattle Times ran numerous articles about Germany. It brought together responses to the happenings there. A portion of the articles expresses a fervor feeling, whereas some convey the news with a more flawed subtlety.

In The Times' article on March 23 named "Hitler Granted 4-Year Term as Supreme Ruler," Hitler was quoted as saying that "No enormous upheaval of comparative measurements has been completed with such unvarying control thus little carnage as our revolution." The reason for Hitler's announcement is self-evident: to promise the world that he was administering for the individuals, and there was little requirement for viciousness. Nonetheless, The Times' inclusion started to scrutinize Hitler's declaration. Close to March's furthest limit, there was a bounty of articles distributed concerning the treatment of Jews in Germany. On the 24th, articles ran named "England Roused by Reports of Nazi Violence" and "Eastern Jews Face Expulsion from Germany."

Two days after the fact, on the 26th, articles were distributed with the titles "[British] Jews Boycott German Goods," and "Abuse of Jews not allowed." The titles alone were disturbing and offered a lie to Hitler's previous announced declarations of harmony. Not exclusively did the titles of these articles communicate something specific. However, the way that they were gathered in the same spot (inside the particular issue) likewise demonstrated The Times' acknowledgment of an example of occasions.

Similarly, as the reportage began to incline toward questions about Hitler, the readers of The Seattle Times were, by and by, consoled: It was around the same time that articles about Jewish oppression got out in the media. On March 26, there was another article titled "Hitler Praised." This article accounted for that "Washington copyist's interruption to offer recognition of remark to Herr Hitler, Germany's bubbly Chancellor." It countered any disquiet that may have been from updates on Jewish mistreatment and isolated Hitler's authority from Germany's infringements on its Jewish and dissenter residents' freedoms. By utilizing a word like bubbly, which has an exceptionally sure implication, this article's writer drove the reader to consider decidedly for Adolf Hitler. The Seattle Times likewise distributed articles that appeared to console the reader about the earlier day's news: "Germany Tells US Catholics That Jews Are Safe." The article expressed that the German Foreign Minister told the Cardinal of Boston that, to the extent of the supposed abuse of German Jews, "I ask to guarantee your greatness that such charges are without all foundation." In the following day's publication, The Seattle Times ventured to such an extreme as to proclaim that "there is no sorted out abuse of Jews in Germany" and "In our nation, at any rate, the official offices of government are solid and fair: their affirmation that there has been no racial mistreatment in Germany and will be none might depend upon." Once more, The Seattle Times was consoling its readers, in the wake of distributing articles concerning barbarities, that everything was okay in Germany, and there was no compelling reason to stress.

The example of announcing the Nazi's constraint of Jews close by consoling articles continued all through the spring. A couple of days after this publication guaranteeing that there was "no racial oppression," The Times' March 31st feature read: "Nazis Expel Jewish Judges." The informative first-page article was titled "Hitler War on Judah to Be Drastic, Universal: Virtual Extermination of Race from Economic Life of Reich Starts in Earnest Tomorrow Morning." This article clarified that the Nazis had restricted all protesters (Jews, Communists, and Marxists) from proficient criminal courts. Suppressing the nonconformists was a stage toward complete restraint. It ought to have been very troubling for the residents of Seattle as they were watching these situations develop, particularly when reading the line: "new government announcement... characterized the activity against Jews as the start of a war on the whole Jewish race of the world."

A few issues in April featured news with these worries of constraint, while different articles asserted precisely the opposite. An April 1 article revealed the start of the Jewish boycott started in Germany, during which Germans boycotted Jewish work environments with a sentence that read, "There were such numerous appalling perspectives to the situation." The word shocking has a definite negative meaning and was undoubtedly startling to the reader. An article in the April 3 issue supported this unpropitious impact, declaring that "starting noon no one will be permitted to leave German soil without uncommon permission." This occasion made protesters, for example, Jews, detainees of their legislature. However, regardless of its dismal tone, this article did not have incredible accentuation. It nearly appeared as though The Seattle Times did not have the foggiest idea what to think about this news, and accordingly, the reader would have been in a comparable situation.

Another powerful article in the April 7 issue featured these disparities between the news The Seattle Times revealed and its general article trust in Hitler's system. The article was a letter from a reader titled "Our Woeful Ignorance."

The writer contended that "In an ongoing issue of The Times, there seemed a publication named 'No Persecution,' the essayist of which demonstrated a level of trust in Adolf Hitler." They proceeded to ask, "Does the Times for a second expect that the German government would concede that there was any sorted-out abuse or that our discretionary delegates to Berlin would be educated regarding what is happening behind the scenes?" Moreover, at long last closed, "To state that Hitler would not permit any composed oppression of the Jews shows that the author of the article is woefully uninformed of the historical backdrop of German politics." It was a significant article in The Times since it was composed by a reader who unequivocally called attention to the conflicting inclusion of The Seattle Times. The writer attempted to open the eyes of readers of The Seattle Times, to what was truly going on and maybe increase the feeling of dread toward the Nazis.

Regardless of this current reader's dissent letter, The Seattle Times distributed articles of comparative tone. For instance, an article on April 23 pardoned fascisms as "Simple Interludes," or "compromise[s] between wavering, often wasteful however consistently esteemed mainstream rule and the organization of monarchy." On the 23rd was a whole page containing a meeting with Emil Lengyel, the writer of a book called Hitler. In this meeting, "Mr. Lengyel... does not accept that Hitler... will start as rough a program as certain individuals dread. He accepts that Hitler will give Germany an administration that will not go amiss a long way from the center course." Both of these articles conveyed a tone of consolation. It appeared like The Times was endeavoring to forestall such a frenzy in Seattle by distributing consoling news, just as minimizing the size of the Nazi's restraint, potentially out of an absence of worry for Jewish individuals.

On May 16, the feature read "Incapacitate, Roosevelt Pleads!" Although the article expressed that Roosevelt did not name a specific nation, he was predominantly coordinating this supplication toward German militarism. After two days, following their past example, The Times printed an article keeping up the faith in Nazi Germany's serene desire. The article, named "All Germany to Backing Hitler in Peace Stand," expressed that "the entire German country energized today behind the legislature in seriousness guaranteeing the world that she consecrated goals are elusive peace." In a specific sense, The Times' inclusion was following Hitler's political developments, he did nothing he would nation administrator, nations abusive and threatening acts with explanations of his group's tranquil and authentic expectations. It continued: on May 30, there was an article titled: "Germany Says 'Hands Off' on Jewish Policy." Hitler requested the League of Nations to "keep its hands off the subject of Germany's treatment of the Jews." Anyone reading this article would have been extremely dubious of this announcement to make a "do ask-don't tell" demeanor towards the Nazi treatment of the Jews. More articles written about the inescapable restraint of Hitler's system got out throughout the following four months.

In the long stretches of June, July, August, and September, Hitler started to utilize his extremist muscles truly. On June 19, in an article titled "Nazi Government May Rear

Children," there was a statement that said, "Hitler has harshly cautioned German guardians that their youngsters will be removed and put under the administration's wing if they are not raised to be notable Nazis."

Then, on August 14, a man from the United States was condemned to a six-month jail term for supposedly considering Hitler, a Czech Jew. Similarly, on August 19, an article was distributed titled "When in Berlin Do as Nazis Do," recounting the narrative of another American man attacked by Hitler's soldiers in Berlin for neglecting to salute Nazi soldiers walking through the town. Lastly, an article written on September 1, named "Hitler Greeted like King at Nazi Congress." These articles imparted away from the individuals of Seattle about Hitler's expectations in Germany and worldwide. If there were any questions regarding whether Hitler would administer with an "iron clench hand," they would have been answered by the late spring's news inclusion. The most recent couple of long periods of 1933 shows such activity.

For quite a long time, the USSR had been in talks with Britain and France, who had sworn to protect Poland if Germany attacked, to shape a three-path union against Nazi animosity. Germany and the USSR, notwithstanding, had consented to a financial arrangement the day before. Presently Hitler needed a political settlement thought Molotov said he "energetically invited." With fight readiness plans on hold as the European forces considered shaping a unified front against Germany, Hitler could not shroud his desperation. "The pressure among Germany and Poland has gotten grievous," he cautioned Stalin. "An emergency may emerge quickly."

At last, Stalin's reaction showed up 27 hours after the fact: Send Ribbentrop to Moscow.

On August 23, 1939, Ribbentrop showed up with composed requests close by Hitler to arrange. Such a discretionary invasion would have been unbelievable just a short time previously. The Nazis and Soviets had been mortal foes on opposite sides of the philosophical range who utilized each other's scorn to fuel their dangerous systems. Presently, Realpolitik bested philosophy. After the Germans accused Czechoslovakia earlier in the year infringing upon the Munich Agreement, Stalin scrutinized the purpose of the British and French to battle the Nazis. The Soviets, then, discovered a harmony with the Germans appealing given that they were at that point occupied with a furious fight on their eastern front with the Japanese, and the Red Army was as yet debilitated from Stalin's purge of its top authorities in 1937 and 1938.

So abrupt was the defrost between them that the five insignia banners raced to the air terminal to welcome Ribbentrop upon his appearance had to be taken from Soviet film studios creating anti-Nazi films. When situated at the arranging table inside the Kremlin, the unfamiliar German priest proposed a grandiose introduction about the nations' warm relations. Even an extremist tyrant realized that reality must be twisted in a specific way before it snapped. "The Soviet government could not unexpectedly present to the public affirmations of fellowship after they had been secured with buckets of compost by the Nazi government for a long time," Stalin stated, as per William Shirer's The Rise and Fall of the Third Reich.

While Soviet dealings with the British and French had been delayed for quite a long time, it took only hours to pound out an arrangement with the Germans. The gathering "started and finished energetically, just to show how professional these despots are," the New York Times editorialized. Authoritatively called the Molotov-Ribbentrop Pact, known as the Hitler-Stalin Pact, the peace understanding was raw and explicit. The two nations vowed for a long time "to halt from any demonstration of viciousness, any forceful activity and any assault on one another, either exclusively or together with different forces."

As a vast surrounded photo of Vladimir Lenin looked down harshly upon the smoke-occupied room, Ribbentrop and Molotov joined their signatures to the understanding. A grinning Stalin was as bubbly as the Crimean shining wine that he brought up in an unconstrained toast to Hitler. "I know how much the German country adores its Fuhrer," he said. "I should accordingly prefer to toast his health."

The understanding produced results in the second pen contacted the paper, a rare conciliatory condition that reflected precisely how surged Hitler felt. Ribbentrop called a restless Hitler at his mountain retreat in Bavaria with the news. "That will hit like a stunner," said a delighted Hitler, who could now attack Poland unafraid of a Soviet intercession and a two-front war that had decimated Germany in World War I

"The vile news broke upon the world like a blast," Winston Churchill later composed. Also, that was only the news the world thought about, for notwithstanding the peace agreement, the Nazis and Soviets went into a mystery convention that just reached light after the end of World War II. The two nations took a cutting blade to Poland, with the Germans taking the more significant western cut.

Before Ribbentrop left the Kremlin, Stalin pulled him aside. "The Soviet Government pays attention to the new settlement exceptionally," the despot stated, and he could ensure on his "promise of honor that the Soviet Union would not deceive its accomplice." Stalin more likely than not contemplated whether Hitler felt the same, given the Chancellor's readiness to consent to all Soviet requests just as his sequential propensity for breaking arrangements.

"Our settlement implies that the best European forces have consented to dispose of the danger of war and to live in harmony," Molotov told the Supreme Soviet before it collectively approved the agreement on the night of August 31. Hours after the fact, over a million German soldiers crossed the fringe with Poland. World War II had started. Inside weeks, the Soviets invaded eastern Poland under the pretense of shielding its occupants from the Germans. Months after the fact, Stalin's soldiers walked into the Baltics and Bessarabia.

Before the signing of the peace settlement, President Franklin D. Roosevelt cautioned Stalin that "it was as sure as the night followed the day that when Hitler had vanquished France he would turn on Russia and it would be the Soviets' chance straightaway." The words were farsighted when on June 22, 1941, Hitler singularly broke his agreement with Stalin and dispatched the biggest assault throughout the entire history of war.

The Legion Freies Indien, alluded to casually as the Indische Legion ("Indian Legion"), differently referred to likewise as the Tiger Legion and the Azad Hind Fauj (Hindi: "Free India Army"), was an Indian military unit raised during World War II in Germany. It was first brought up in 1941 and joined the German Army (Wehrmacht Heer) and later, from August 1944, appended to the Waffen-SS. The Army was to fill in as an Indian freedom force. It was brought about by Subhas Chandra Bose, director of the Indian National Congress and a noticeable pioneer of the Indian autonomy development, who helped to establish the Army when he came to Berlin in 1941, having gotten away from British house arrest in India. The enlisted soldiers were Indian understudy volunteers living in Germany at that time, and a small bunch from the Indian prisoners of war (POWs) caught by Erwin Rommel during his North Africa Campaign. It would later draw a more significant number of Indian

POWs as volunteers.

Even though it was an attacking bunch that would frame a pathfinder to a German-Indian joint intrusion of British India's western boondocks, hundreds of the legionnaires were dropped into eastern Iran in 'Activity Bajadere' to invade India through Baluchistan and cause harm against the British in anticipation of a foreseen public revolt. Most Indian Legion soldiers were just ever positioned in Europe – generally in non-battle obligations – from the Netherlands to Atlantic Wall obligations in France until France's Allied invasion. A little unforeseen, including the administration and the officer corps, was moved to Azad Hind ("Free India") after its arrangement and saw activity in the INA's Burma Campaign. In Italy, the unit saw activity against British and Polish soldiers and embraced the enemy of sectarian tasks in 1944.

At the Third Reich surrender in 1945, the rest of the Indian Legion soldiers attempted to walk to impartial Switzerland over the Alps. However, these endeavors became useless as American and French soldiers caught them and, in the long run, sent them back to India to deal with indictments of treason.

Due to the mayhem, the preliminaries of Indians who fought with the Axis caused among regular people and the military of British India, the Indian Legion individuals' preliminaries were incomplete.

The Third Reich was a police state described by self-assertive capture and detainment of political and philosophical adversaries in inhumane imprisonments.

With the reevaluation of "defensive care" (Schutzhaft) in 1933, police power got free of legal controls. In Nazi wording, defensive care implied the capture—without legal justification—of the system's genuine and expected rivals. "Defensive guardianship" detainees were not limited to the common jail framework yet in death camps under the SS's selective authority (Schutzstaffel, the first-class watchmen of the Nazi state).

Jewish legal advisors lined up to apply for consent to show up under the Berlin courts' watchful eye. Jewish attorneys lined up to apply for authorization to show up under the Berlin courts' watchful eye.

New guidelines set out in the Aryan Paragraph (a progression of laws ordered in April 1933 to remove Jews from different circles of State and society) permitted just 35 to show up under the watchful eye of the court. Berlin, Germany, April 11, 1933.

The Third Reich has been known as a double state since the typical legal framework coincided with Hitler and the police's subjective intensity. However, as most public life zones after the Nazi ascent to control in 1933, the German arrangement of equity went through "coordination" (arrangement with Nazi objectives). All expert affiliations associated with the equity organization converged into the

National Socialist League of German Jurists. In April 1933, Hitler passed one of the most punctual xenophobic laws, removing Jewish and Socialist appointed authorities, legal advisors, and other court officials from their jobs. Further, the Academy of German Law and Nazi legitimate scholars, for example, Carl Schmitt, upheld the Nazification of German law, purging it of "Jewish impact." Judges were ordered to let "sound society assumption" (gesundes Volksempfinden) direct them in their choices.

Hitler resolved to expand the political dependability of the courts. In 1933 he built up superior courts all through Germany to hear politically delicate cases. Disappointed with the 'not blameworthy' decisions delivered by the Supreme Court (Reichsgericht) in the Reichstag Fire Trial, Hitler requested the formation of the People's Court (Volksgerichtshof) in Berlin in 1934 to attempt conspiracy and other significant "political cases." Under Roland Freisler, the People's Court turned out to be essential for the Nazi arrangement of dread, denouncing countless individuals as "Volk Vermin" and thousands more to death for "Volk Treason." The preliminary and condemning of those blamed for complicity in the July Plot, the endeavor to execute Hitler in July 1944, was incredibly unreasonable.

The facts demonstrate that a backhanded change of the constitution, by a revising rule alone, was admissible without consolidating all the while or then again later the adjustment expected by the resolution in the constitution's content. Notwithstanding, the Enabling Act was not just a correction of one or a few provisos of the constitution. It added up to a total topple of the established order at that point existing. An essential modification of the whole sacred structure, a "complete amendment" in the French and Swiss statute feeling, is past the ordinary changing organs' ward. It said "first constituent intensity of the whole German nation."'" Although most of the sacred legal advisors before 1933, excusing this qualification among customary and essential adjustments of the constitution, kept up the pertinence of Article 7620 for all revisions at all. It is unnoticeable that the National Socialist faction spoke to just a minority. Even by including the votes of its accomplice, the German National People's Party, it remained extensively underneath the all-around acknowledged level for an altering dominant part.

Another test to the dependability of the Enabling Act is even more genuine. It was passed by a 494-94 vote in the Reichstag, subsequently adjusting officially to Article 76 of the constitution. However, 81 agents of the prohibited Communist faction were not allowed to gather and 120 individuals from the Social Democrats. Twenty-one also, 92 individuals from the Catholic Center, the Social Democrats, and minor "splinter parties" deciding in favor of the demonstration were kept from giving a free and fair vote. The crowd released by the Government entered the legislative hall, and the vote was in an unbelievable climate of scare tactic and intimidation.

The last point bearing basically on the legality of future enactment based on the Enabling Act is the most significant. The act pronounced in Article 5: "Moreover, this demonstration stops to be powerful at the point when another supplants the current legislature of the Reich."

On June 29, 1933, Dr. Hugenberg, Minister of Nutrition and Agriculture, left the bureau under tension. By the German National People's Party's preeminent agent's withdrawal, the alliance was the Government's idea and was not accepted. That is because the German Nationals' help had the National Socialists achieved the majority share of votes and seats. After the abdication of the alliance accomplice, the bureau of Hitler protected its real personality; what is more, that no new bureau could come. However, the circumstance's core was not unique about that under the Enabling Act of 1923. The Enabling Act forces have concurred to an alliance government, which all things considered had gotten the parliamentary order. After the abdication of the German Nationals, followed quickly by the concealment of the gathering itself, the bureau's political character was, in a general sense, changed.

By no more significant thoughts might it be able to be kept up that the general forces of the demonstration were given to the National Socialists alone since the presence of the German Nationals in the legislature was considered by all groups deciding in favor of the go about as such a political brake. Consequently, the demonstration lost its political premise and, in this way, likewise its legitimacy.

Chapter four

Trade and Commerce

Germany had a significant influence on the breaking down of worldwide international finance and exchange during the 1930s. Squeezed by interminable current account shortfalls and driven by a belief system that planned to build up authority over Europe, Nazi Germany diverted its foreign exchange and monetary relations into an inflexible arrangement of reciprocal exchange and clearing arrangements. Contemporary eyewitnesses, just as later academic examination have asserted that during the 1930s, Germany effectively equipped this framework towards the financial abuse of its exchanging partners. Hirschman called attention to Germany being regularly the biggest exchanging accomplice of the smaller European nations and summed up this into a hypothesis of imposing business model force in global exchange. Afterward, Child investigated the common clearing framework and guaranteed that Germany mishandled these game plans to separate both money related and genuine assets from its smaller trading partners. These more established discussions created a universality that continued for decades.

An elective point of view that has recently picked up acknowledgment was created by Neal, who saw that the terms of exchange understood Germany's exchanging courses of action were not one-sided towards German preferred position. The proof found by Neal appeared to square well with a political point of view from Milward, who had contended that by putting assets to develop its casual financial realm during the 1930s, Germany yielded transient monetary advantage. More recently, Kitson contended from assessing the German foreign exchange structure before the war that Germany relinquished terms of exchange preferences for political impact. This contention has been received additionally by Feinstein, Temin, and Toniolo in their reading material record of the European economy between the wars. What the current writing shares is an absence of quantitative proof adequate to set up some point. As the Nazi organization kept the necessary information on the equalization of installments mystery from 1936, just the unfamiliar exchange insights are accessible from distributed hotspots for the last part of the 1930s.

Rich information base on the different segments of the equalization of installments has been made due in the chronicles; furthermore, tiny segments are in later factual work. Given that this is unequivocally the time length for which the distributed sources give just unfamiliar exchange measurements. The extra component secured by the unpublished material incorporates the missing parts of the parity of installments, such as moves and capital developments. It also incorporates the parities of unfamiliar trade expenses and receipts by nation, separated by balance-of-payments classifications and exchanges on clearing account contrasted and foreign convertible trade. Investigating this information makes it conceivable to acquire a rich image of the exchange and installment streams of Nazi Germany before the Second World War. Assessment of these and integral sources on German foreign exchange and trade approaches not long before the Second World War loans backing to the later commitments to the discussion referenced previously. The outcomes recommend that an unfamiliar exchange strategy alone was not adequate for Germany to misuse the little. As a standard, abuse seems to have started simply after a given nation's military control, however, then for a considerable scope.

The Third Reich is not only an autocracy but also a kleptocracy. Hitler's standard put together not merely concerning fascism, also on loot, burglary, and plundering. It is critical to perceive not because it adds another measurement to National Socialism violations but because it causes us to see how the Third Reich functioned.

They started at an opportune time. In 1923 Hitler sent his stormtroopers to plunder a Jewish bank to get reserves. Later on, until 1933, he stopped such activities. However, in 1933 they were again given free rein. Massive plundering of worker's organization premises began on May 2, 1933, when furniture, utensils, even beds were removed. Assaults on Jewish temples and the demolition of 7,500 Jewish shops and the destruction of a considerable number of Jewish houses happened on the purported Reichskristallnacht on 9-10 November 1938, joined by the robbery or evacuation of numerous individual belongings and assets of the proprietors. Following the Anschluss in

March 1938, the Nazis tossed Jewish occupants out of their homes and plundered the remains; Jews were halted in the city and looted of their fur garments, gems, and wallets.

Such plundering withered into unimportance in contrast with the methodical appropriation of Jewish resources, starting very quickly on the Nazi seizure of power in 1933. An assortment of legitimate instruments, including department store chains, shops and other organizations were targeted. Run of the mill – Heydrich's Devisenfahndungsamt (1936) could bring organizations into an organization if they were there to help get capital out of Germany – produced admissions, created cross-examination records. Territorial Economic Consultants' workplaces of the Nazi Party selected trustees to Jewish firms, and utilized an April 7, 1933 law to dispose of Jewish supervisors and proprietors. The Four Year Plan utilized demanding forces. The movement expanded after Reichskristallnacht when the government officially requested the assignment or Aryanization of Jewish owned or run organizations. The night before the war, no Jewish owned or ran organizations left.

Perhaps around one-fifth of purchase outs were completed by companions or supporters at a reasonable cost or on excellent standing. Approximately 40 percent paid the base permitted, for example, excluding 'generosity' because as far as anyone knows, there was none; 40 percent viably constrained, utilizing coercion, Gestapo and some of the time open savagery. There were numerous benefits – for example, NS Regional Economic Offices took a 10% commission on the price tag of Jewish organizations; in Thuringia, the NS Regional Economic Officer made more than a million checks like this and utilized it to purchase up organizations himself.

It gave scenery to monstrous Jewish resources' plunder during the war; such activity reached Polish property. On September 27, 1939, Poland's German military government announced a sweeping reallocation of Polish property, affirming the request again on October 5, 1939. On October 19, 1939, Göring reported that the Four-Year Plan's Office held onto all Polish and Jewish property in the consolidated domains. A pronouncement formalized this on September 17, 1940, that set up a focal organization, the Haupttreuhandstelle Ost, to oversee the seized property. In February 1941, these effectively included more than 205,000 organizations extending in size from little workshops to major modern undertakings. By June 1941, 50 percent of business and 33% of the bigger landed Reich Trustees had taken over homes in the attached regions without remuneration. These requests, in actuality, comprised a permit to any Germans to plunder what they needed. Likewise, the military assumed control over a significant number of homesteads to make sure about food supplies for the soldiers.

The German intruders additionally carted away vast amounts of social goods. During an assault on the Bernadin religious community in Radeczina in November 1939, 'all the gold and gem votives were "appropriated,"' as

Klukowski recorded. It was just one of many such occurrences. Nation houses along the attack course occurred, and pressure was applied to their refined proprietors to uncover the whereabouts of concealed fortunes. Before long, the cycle of social seizure was put on a formal basis.. On December 16, 1939, the German specialists requested the mandatory enlistment of everything equal and social articles dating from before 1850, along with jewelry, instruments, coins, books, and furniture.

An official chief, Kajetan Mühlmann, who had recently completed comparative obligations in Vienna, was responsible for the cycle. Before the finish of November 1940, the enrollment finished, and Hitler's craft operator Hans Posse showed up to choose prime examples for Hitler.

He was followed at the appropriate time by artistry historical center chiefs from Germany. Fights broke out, as Hermann Göring attempted to acquire pictures for himself while Hans Frank had a problem with the removal of prize plunder from his central command. Maybe this was not such an impractical notion, notwithstanding, since Frank had no clue about how to show or protect Old Masters, and was once criticized by Mühlmann for draping an artwork by Leonardo da Vinci over a radiator. Private assortments were just as state historical centers, and the tremendous assortment amassed by the Czartoryski family, including a Rembrandt and a Raphael, was deliberately raided.

In the interim, Hans Frank designed his base camp with plundered fine arts and transportation trophies back to Bavaria. When American soldiers showed up there in 1945, they found a Rembrandt, a Leonardo, a fourteenth-century Madonna from Cracow, and plundered garments and goblets from Polish chapels. He even alluded to himself as a looter nobleman. He appropriated the bequest of the Potocki family for use as a provincial retreat and drove around his fiefdom in a limousine sufficiently huge to pull in remarks even from partners, for example, the Governor of Galicia. Aping Hitler, he fabricated an impersonation of Hitler's Berghof in the slopes near Zakopane. He arranged radiant meals, which made his waistline extend so quickly that he counseled a dietician since he could scarcely fit into his dress uniform anymore.

Simultaneously, ordinary Poles' states of life were getting progressively worse, as food supplies became all the more scant. Plundering and confiscation continued. Seizures discarded to social items, however, included, for instance, the removal of gear from college research facilities for use in Germany. Indeed, even the Warsaw Zoo's assortment of toys was not available. As in the Reich itself for quite a while, iron and steel objects, for example, leave railings and nursery entryways, even candelabras and pots were there to be melted down and used in deadly weapon and vehicle creation in Germany. At the point when the virus winter truly started to chomp, in January 1940, the clinic chief Dr. Zygmunt Klukowski noticed, 'the German police took all sheepskin coats from passing locals and left them just in coats.' A short time later, the occupation powers started attacking towns and appropriating all the banknotes they discovered there—comparative activities during and after USSR intrusion in June 1942.

There was an explanation behind this. To begin with, Jews and Poles were thought of assub-par. Hitler's plan was to wreck Polish culture, and execute Polish scholars. Second, there was a definite inclination among Nazis that Jews specifically had taken things from the Germans in any case, through misuse and 'profiteering.' Neither Jews nor Poles were truly refined; they did not merit all the social articles they previously possessed. At last, this had become an ordinary piece of financial life in the Third Reich; thus, it started in Poland and the USSR.

In any case, there were different thought processes, as well. The critical factor was the extra-lawful premise of Hitler's power. What Hitler said and did was law. This 'right' state broadened right down the progression to what individuals regularly alluded to as the 'little Hitler's,' the neighborhood party supervisors, and even grassroots party individuals. Disdain for law was virtually apparent in the 1920s. Insofar as it did not repudiate essential fundamentals of Nazi philosophy, extra-lawful conduct endured, if it could advocate for the sake of National Socialism.

Furthermore, the Reichstag and authoritative gatherings were quiet, the press and media assumed responsibility for the Propaganda Ministry, and the justice administration and police powers were completely Nazified.

Everyday gathering, individuals expected compensations under the Third Reich for their sufferings in the supposed "season of battle." It was a compelling method for solidifying the inward union of the gathering, building groups inside it, and making cozy connections of joint commitment among pioneers and devotees at each level.

Likewise, the age of youthful Germans to whom numerous dynamic Nazis had a place, conceived somewhere in the range of 1900 and 1910. It had an upset relationship with cash and financial integrity, having experienced childhood in the denied long periods of the war, having seen cash lose its worth stupendously during the inflation of 1922-23. However, having survived the febrile years, with its legendary instances of defilement and culpability, was deified in Christopher Isherwood's "Mr. Norris Changes Trains."

Afterward, having been pushed into the joblessness and dejection of the Depression from 1929 onwards, it was no big surprise they had no doubts in holding onto what they considered their due when the second came.

As on account of the Jews and Poles, debasement and loot could likewise be how the Nazis embarrassed their adversaries, devastating them by inciting in them a feeling of barrenness as they lost their positions and their assets.

As the Nazis came to power in a nation with a joblessness rate of well over 30%, the primary thing lower positioning storm troopers and gathering individuals anticipated was a vocation. In July 1933, Rudolf Hess guaranteed an occupation to every individual who hosted been a get-together part since before January 30, 1933. In October, the administration formally sorted out work arrangements for individuals with an enrollment number under 300,000 (for example, late 1930) and individuals from the SS, SA, and Stahlhelm who had joined before January 30, 1933.

By 1937 the Reich Post Office had given more than 30,000 positions to 'meriting National Socialists.' By October 1933, the Berlin party had just found employment for 30,000 individuals. Ninety percent of all recently accessible middle-class occupations in the public division went to 'old contenders.' Many were made accessible by excusals under the law of April 7, 1933. Numerous Nazis previously had positions; however, they utilized this strategy to improve their position. Length of gathering enrollment included in computing status, so there were better advancement possibilities. Regularly the positions were not so much required. A review of the Hamburg Sickness Fund in 1934 discovered it had utilized 228 directors, many more directors than it genuinely required. Nearby railroad framework took on over 1,000 new workers in 1933-34. Regularly new occupants were deemed unsatisfactory for occupations to which they delegated. Many people nearly took the pay without trying to go to work.

Theft is successive. Friedrich Stäbel, the new head of public understudies' association since Sept. 1933, purchased vehicles, garments for himself with association reserves, and even utilized a walking band for his entertainment. The line was attracted when it came to party posts, of which there were additionally numerous new ones from 1933 on, as gathering enrollment soared into the millions after the seizure of power. From January 1, 1934, to December 31, 1941, there were almost 11,000 court arraignments for misappropriation of gathering reserves.

However, in numerous parts of the Nazi forces, contraption debasement proceeded unchecked. Especially famous was the Labor Front. Tremendous association, covering essentially totally utilized individuals, supplanting Trade Unions, with an enormous number of workers, all previous worker's guild properties, plus various business activities. Its development division was driven by Anton Karl, who had feelings for robbery and theft dating from the 1920s; he offered more than 580,000 Reichsmarks in incentives in 1936-7 alone to make sure about agreements. Karl sent endowments to anybody he thought significant: the pioneer of Hitler's protector got silk shirts, chasing weapons, and a vacation in Italy for his better half. It also appropriately remunerated Karl with the agreement to remake his unit's sleeping enclosure in Berlin. In 1935 the Labor Front gave Hitler's auxiliaries, just as his picture taker, 20,000 imprints as a Christmas present. As a spy revealing for the restricted SPD noticed, 'the defilement in the Labor Front is tremendous, and the overall norm of ethics correspondingly low.'

It applied especially to the Labor Front's pioneer Robert Ley, whose compensation for this post, at 4,000

Reichsmarks a year, was increased by another 2,000 Reichsmarks as Reich Organization Leader of the Party, 700 RM as a Reichstag representative, and 400 RM as a Prussian State Councilor. The Labor Front put in mass requests for his books and handouts, and he earned 50,000 RM a year from the paper he altered. His diversion costs were paid by the Labor Front, which additionally kept up his manor in Berlin's luxurious Grunewald locale until 1938. He went on a voyage planned by the Labor Front, the travel industry and culture division, known as Strength Through Joy, on another boat named, unavoidably, the Robert Ley. He was joined by a gathering of blonde, blue-eyed young ladies for 'friendship,' and had to be flanked by two mariners each time he showed up at hand to ensure he did not fall off the boat.

Other Nazi pioneers were not far behind Ley in feathering their own nests. Hermann Göringburned through 15 million RM on repairing his lodge, which cost an additional 500,000 RM of citizens' cash in upkeep consistently. He had six further lodges, a château, an Alpine chalet, an estate in Berlin, and a private train, with space for ten cars and a working bread shop to fulfill his craving for cream cakes. The citizen forked out another 1.32 million RM on revamping the train even without the lavish decorations and fittings. To ensure the taxman did not look too carefully at Göring and other Nazi pioneers' undertakings, the legislature decided in 1939 that their duty was to assess workplaces in either Berlin or Munich, which with Nazi authorities who might choose not to see any inconsistencies.

There were numerous famous jokes about Nazi debasement. A 'traditionalist' is 'somebody who has a generously compensated activity that a Nazi likes the appearance of.' Two Nazi authorities are strolling along the street when one of them sees a 50-Reichsmark note and gets it. "I will give it to the Party's Winter Aid program," he says. "Why do it the long way around?" his companion answers – "simply set it on the right track into your pocket." The cabarets Wilhelm Finck was sent to a death camp for making a wisecrack in 1934, when he remained on the phase of Berlin's Catacomb club with his correct arm brought up in a Nazi salute and a tailor estimating him for another suit. "What kind of coat should it be?" asked the tailor. "With pockets fully open, in the current style," Finck answered.

One driving Nazi, nonetheless, was absolved from mainstream dissatisfaction with regards to this sort. Hitler himself delighted in notoriety for integrity, even Puritanism. Unmarried, a veggie-lover, nondrinker, and non-smoker, he extended a picture of yielding private joy for Germany. Another joke had the offspring of Joseph Goebbels, the Propaganda Minister, going round for tea to the homes of Göring, Ley, and other driving Party figures. After each visit, they return home raving about the cream cakes, desserts, and different treats.

After a visit to Hitler, nonetheless, where they get malt espresso and a couple of little, straight rolls, they ask their dad: "Isn't a Führer an individual from the Party, at that point?"

Hitler strengthened his morally right picture by freely denying his compensation as Reich Chancellor, which came to 45,000 Reichsmarks a year, and his yearly costs stipend, which went to another 18,000. The public was not told, in any case, that he had never settled any assessment, nor that when the Munich charge office endeavored to slap a bill of 400,000 Reichsmarks on him falling behind financially in 1934, the thoughtless authorities got a tranquil visit from the Gestapo, after which they discounted the entire whole and wrecked Hitler's duty documents into the deal. Consequently, a thankful Hitler gave the head of the Munich charge office a tax-exempt yearly compensation supplement of 2,000 Reichsmarks for his administrations.

Hitler's genuine pay originated from deals of Mein Kampf, mass purchased by Nazi Party associations, and adding up to 1.2 million Reichsmarks in 1933 alone. From 1937 onwards, he earned tremendous amounts from the copyright charge demanded on the utilization of his representation on postage stamps (50 million Reichsmarks in one year alone); expenses and sovereignties on each printing of any of his addresses in the press.

The heritages left to him by the Adolf Hitler Donation of German Industry; and after Hindenburg's death in 1934, from the President's official assets, which were presently eliminated from the common help evaluating methodology. It permitted him to develop a state subsidize for his removal that, by 1942, had arrived at the astounding total of 24 million imprints.

Hitler utilized this first to offer annuities to older supremacists and hostile to Semitic scholars he portrayed as Nazi 'antecedents', at that point to more than 100 Nazi activists. They had been detained in the Weimar Republic, and afterward, significantly, to the military, basically adulterating its driving commanders to convince them not to embrace any activity against the system. He gave them military works of art for the regimental base camp, he paid 100,000 Reichsmarks a year for officials to go on 'rest fixes,' he expanded the annuities of resigned officials, he furnished Field Marshal von Mackensen with a tax-exempt endowment of a landed bequest along with 350,000 Reichsmarks to take care of redesign expenses. He rehashed this sort of signal with other blue-blooded landowners who craved for the arrival of the Kaiser. Hitler's largesse turned out to be significantly more liberal during the war, when he gave the commanders blessings of cash, works of art, property, and considerably more. Simultaneously, fast advancement, the formation of various new commanders, and Field-Marshals got its prizes the quickly expanding pay rates. Hitler added great month to month increases to the compensations of senior clergymen and authorities, he gave his preferred stone worker Arno Breker a fourth of a million Reichsmarks as a present in 1940, and as a rule, he spread his gifts around vast pieces of the military, ecclesiastical, shared help, and social elites. Subsequently, one of the significant and often disregarded elements holding the highest levels of the Nazi Party together was defilement: the receipt of huge blessings, tremendous increments in pay, property. That solidified the support relationship they had with Hitler in a relationship of clientage that, at that point, rehashed itself for a little scope right down the chain of command to the base.

During the war, the expansion of defilement went inseparably with a proportionate increment in the scale and power of loot, plundering, and theft, as have already been mentioned on Poland's account. The equivalent was false in nations like France, Denmark, or Italy.

Hitler and Göring had no doubts about securing artistry objects for their collections, specifically for Hitler's arranged craftsmanship exhibition hall in his old neighborhood of Linz, from significant collections there, and as everyday environments crumbled in involved towns.

German officials and overseers were often ready to gobble up artistry objects at very discounted costs from urgent Belgians or Dutchmen searching for cash to spare themselves from starving.

The elimination of Europe's Jews started in the second half of 1941 and brought Jewish resources under the control of Nazis, whether through the reallocation of their property and their organizations or the pillaging of their bodies. Major German banks benefitted, for instance, from the extraction of gold fillings from the teeth of dead Jews. The entirety of this went further to add to a familiar feeling of complicity in wrongdoing that was one more factor holding the Nazi force structure's echelons together as the military circumstance weakened.

Plundering and loot additionally had a more extensive task to carry out, nonetheless. As of late, the extreme German antiquarian Götz Aly has contended that it was broad to such an extent that it successfully kept the mass of conventional Germans faithful to the system during the war by keeping up their expectations for everyday comforts at a satisfactory level. Fighters and authorities sent back ordinary parcels of food, shoes, apparel, and more to their families at home. Aly refers to the wartime letters of the later author Heinrich Böll that went with such bundles, with margarine, cheddar, and different groceries that could be bought economically in France yet were hard to obtain in Germany. The food, apparel, furniture, and much else other than that had a place with expelled Jews were appropriated and sent back to Germany efficiently. In the initial three months of 1943, for instance, the soldiers of the Eighteenth armed force on the Leningrad front sent over 3,000,000 packages back home, loaded down with merchandise of numerous sorts, undeniably more than came the other way, despite the apparent multitude of privations the German soldiers were suffering in the Russian winter. There was a thundering exchange in plundered hides, for instance.

For a more significant scope, German companies demanded, purchased up, or nearly seized primary monetary resources in vanquished nations to reinforce the economy back home. These went from constrained takeovers of adversary Western European firms by the synthetics monster I G Farben to the ordering of more than 8,000 railroad cars from the Belgian rail routes by their German partner. Götz Aly indicated that the entirety of this permitted German war ventures to continue onward and, it empowered the German state to keep burdens.

Correspondingly, defilement may have influenced holding the Nazi party and government mechanical assembly together. However, the belief system was significant here as well, maybe considerably more so. If Nazi heads appreciated the material prizes and features of intensity, they none the less held that power in any case because of their philosophical feelings. Most importantly, maybe, it was philosophy, not the need or want for plunder, which fuelled the Nazi approach of eliminating Europe's Jews. It is valid that the Nazis settled on a progression of choices not to squander assets, through their eyes, on taking care of and keeping up the 4,000,000 Soviet detainees of war they caught in 1941-2, or on the millions of additional Jews they captured in Poland, the Ukraine and Belarus. In any case, the essential choice to execute these individuals was a capacity not of monetary need however of belief system: of the Nazis' disdain for what they saw as Slavic subhumans, and, all the more profoundly, of their assurance to free Europe and maybe, at last, the universe of what they considered as a substantial Jewish danger to Germany's presence.

Notwithstanding all the work done over the most recent couple of years, we know very little about the impacts of plundering and loot on the German economy, most notably during the war.

Whatever these were, in any case, the plundering itself was on an enormous enough scale to possess us still more than sixty years after the fact, as the continuation of compensation activities regarding social items and different sorts of property show consistently. Maybe at long last, as well, the impacts of debasement on the Third Reich and how it worked, both at home and abroad, were an uncommon instance of the impacts of unrestricted force by and large. However, it is a platitude; there is no more adequate method of finishing this short talk than to cite Lord Acton, Regius Professor of Modern History: *"Force will work in general degenerate, and total force undermines completely."*

Chapter five

The Jewish Question

In the archives of human atrocities, the Germans' brutalities over the Jews in Nazi Germany are among the most terrible recollected. The Holocaust sticks out so distinctively because it was so all-around recorded. Through film and fastidious records, we have been observers of the Germans' precise mass-murder and their total surrender of empathy. About the disgraceful scar left upon western development, there is no doubt. Notwithstanding, a couple of questions do remain. Why was the Nazi party so alluring to the German public? Were the people of Germany lured by Hitler's unfathomable appeal and mesmerized by the Nazi's constant promulgation, or would they say they were commonly following their wants? Is it because a wellspring of that craving prompted such fierceness?

The Nazi Party was appealing too fast of the German people since Hitler, and his group proposed an answer for practically every difficulty confronting the populace. For instance, the Party plan tended to the issue of Germany's loss of WWI. The Nazis abused the common misconception that Germany's military was "betrayed" by the Weimar Republic's first lawmakers. Along these lines, they tempted the German individuals into associating the loss of the war with Democracy.

Another mainstream objective of the Nazis was to cancel the Treaty of Versailles. This settlement, composed by the Allies after Germany's annihilation in WWI, was intended to humble Germany. Germany needed to annul necessary military help, neutralize the domain on the left bank of the Rhine River, pay an excruciating fine in reparations, surrender its provincial terrains and accept total accountability for beginning the war. This arrangement was incredibly disagreeable among Germans. There were no government officials who might need to be seen as supporting it. However, the Nazi development utilized it as a revitalizing point. Here is an extract from a flyer declaring a Hitler discourse:

Adolf Hitler stands up. Come and dissent against Germany being troubled with the war blame. Dissent against the Peace Treaty of Versailles, which has been constrained upon us by the war's only guilty party, the Jewish worldwide stock trade statehouse. To each German, destroying the deal would bring a feeling of strengthening and rapture. The Nazi party guaranteed a political way to do that.

In many of his discourses during his rise to power, Hitler regularly talked about the "treacherous" disposition of the Weimar government with its strategies of satisfying the deal's terms. On February 24, 1920, in the principal public gathering of the German Worker's Party (later to be named NSDAP), Hitler delineated the gathering program. The main point tended to the idea of a bound together Germany having a ball "assurance." The following point talked legitimately on the Paris Treaty: "We request uniformity of rights for the German people in its dealings with different countries, and annulment of the Peace Treaties of Versailles and St. Germain." Thus, the Nazis embraced a prominent position which would guarantee the German people an approach to work back their nationalistic pride and eliminate the blade from the military's back. Without the deal, Germany could revamp its military, which had consistently assumed a significant function in its personality.

Another explanation the Nazis were so appealing to the German public was the extraordinary financial difficulties after WWI. The hyper-inflation of 1923 forced homemakers to use the worthless German money to ignite fires. With every tough swing of the economy, development in Nazi participation deteriorated.

As the economy collapsed, Nazi enlistment grew. The Nazi's discretionary forward leap in 1932 owed a lot to the 1929 misery whose infection spread worldwide.

The outrageous neediness of the time caused difficulty in rustic networks among ranchers. Generally, a significant part of the town life was full of networks and individuals helping each other. However, the harder it turned out to use money, the more the networks started to separate. Public Socialism had the option to interest these divided networks with blood, land, and public unity ideas.

An engaging property of the Nazi Party to Germany's bourgeois and its tip-top was its opposition to Marxism. In the 1930s, a frantic, urban common was starting to merge with the German Communist and Socialist coalitions. It represented a genuine danger to the center and high society. Hitler made a more forceful development, sorted out and more revolutionary than the furthest left of the Reichstag. The bourgeois and the upper class did not need an upheaval like that of Russia. An extremist state would require its installment, yet it would not request all out redistribution of all private property in any event.

The Nazis spoke to the Germans by fueling the previously existing patterns in hostility to Semitism. The historical backdrop of anti-Semitism is broad in Germany. One source the Nazi development drew upon was a paranoid fear dependent on a publication called "Conventions of the Elders of Zion." This record began in the last part of the 1800s. It illustrated a supposed worldwide scheme to dominate and administer the world. As per Protocols, the Jews planned to utilize different weapons, for example, conjuring the French Revolution, progressivism, communism, Socialism, and political agitation to subvert European culture. As indicated by history specialists for the Encyclopedia of the Holocaust, the record was supposedly fashioned at the hour of the Dreyfus Affair (1894) by Pyotr Ivanovich Rachkovski, head of an unfamiliar part of the Russian secret police situated in Paris. The French Right needed a report that would ensnare Richard Dreyfus in the supposed connivance. The Czar further utilized the convention to help his enemy of Semitic arrangements in Russia. Afterward, the Protocol found its way into Germany. In 1919 and 1923, Alfred Rosenburg, a Nazi ideologist, composed five generally conveyed leaflets about the connivance. Additionally, Julius Streicher's paper, Der Strummer (the aggressor), frequently referred to the conventions.

In his rationale, Hitler accepted that because Jewish pioneers had guaranteed that the Protocols implemented, they absolutely should be valid at that point. Hitler even flaunted that he had gained much from the Protocols about political interest, disguise, redirection, and association strategies. Alfred Rosenburg constructed many ways of thinking about acknowledging the "reality" of the Protocols. These thoughts brought numerous Germans and different Europeans into the Nazi party.

Julius Streicher was a Nazi advocate who made a vocation of advancing enemies of Semitism. He impugned Jews in rough and horrible manners in his notorious paper Der Strummer for a long time. Here is one of the endless examples of Streicher's disdain promulgation:

The family head purges a couple of drops of the new and powdered blood into the glass, wets the left hand's fingers with it and splashes, favors with it, everything on the table. At that point, the head of the family says, 'Hence we request that God send the ten diseases to all adversaries of the Jewish confidence.' Then they eat. Furthermore, toward the end, the head of the family shouts, 'May all Gentiles die, as the kid whose blood contained in the bread and wine.'

Der Strummer was a broadly read weekly paper. Its most striking element was its first-page kids' shows now and then portraying Jews as vampires and attackers.

It was mighty informing German general feeling against the Jews. Streicher likewise composed and distributed a youngsters' book to prepare youth to loathe Jews since the beginning.

Another method for catching the German mind was the idea of an unadulterated race – hereditarily homogenous populaces. The Nazis extended the Aryan standards, which advanced pride in having German blood. The value of being German was expanding because they were generalized as being predominant mentally and truly. They were usually more talented than different races in profound quality also. Apart from the German resident was anticipated, recommending that by their work, if they were men, and by their fruitfulness, the German public could make a compelling society if they were ladies. After encountering the pessimism that was the public state of mind in the 1920s, such oversimplified customary thoughts were very seductive.

The Nazi Party consolidated the issues of Germany's selling out in WWI, the arrangement of Versailles, the Weimar Republic's uncouthness at taking care of the economy, public solidarity, dread of Marxism, anti-Semitism, and the German individuals' ethnic personality into an amazingly made promulgation bundle. Its essential point was to take a shot at the German public's feelings of dread and expectations until the Nazi belief system entranced them. Hitler's true virtuoso laid in his capacity to utilize publicity like a specialist's surgical tool. He realized how to target explicit groups and appeal to them on an emotional level. Since the majority were generally uninformed, this was the place he put forth his most noteworthy attempts. He wrote in Mein Kampf that with the goal for promulgation to be utilized viably, it must to the academic degree of the most restricted: "the more prominent the mass it is proposed to come to, the lower its learned level should be... we should stay away from extreme scholarly requests on our public... " Here we perceive how Hitler's psyche functioned. He focused on the biggest conceivable crowd and custom-made his running stage and promulgation to the most reduced shared element of knowledge. Like this, he caught mass allure and had the option to control the general conclusion.

In 1941, during the USSR's German invasion, the Nazis started their mission of killing vigorously.

Nazi commandants were trying different things with approaches to execute as a once huge mob behind the lines. They expected that shooting individuals would be excessively distressing for their officers, thus thinking of more effective homicide methods.

Exploratory gas vans slaughtered intellectually incapacitated individuals in Poland as early as 1939. The toxic exhaust was siphoned into a fixed compartment to choke out those inside.

Nazis compiled in January 1942 at the Wannsee Conference to arrange what they called a "last answer for the Jewish inquiry" - slaughtering the whole European Jewish population, 11 million individuals, by elimination and constrained work.

What was Auschwitz?

Auschwitz was initially a Polish armed force sleeping enclosure in southern Poland. Nazi Germany attacked and invaded Poland in September 1939, and by May 1940, transformed the site into a prison for political detainees.

With the notorious untruth 'Arbeit Macht Frei' over the passageway in German, this zone means work liberates - it became known as Auschwitz I.

However, as the war and the Holocaust advanced, the Nazi system significantly built up the site.

The first individuals gassed were a gathering of Polish and Soviet detainees in September 1941. Work started on another camp, Auschwitz II-Birkenau, the next month. It turned into the gigantic gas chambers site where several thousand were killed until November 1944, and the crematoria were the place their bodies burned.

German synthetic chemical corporation I.G. Farben constructed and worked an engineered elastic manufacturing plant at Auschwitz III-Monolith. Other privately owned businesses like Krupp and Siemens-Schuckert likewise ran industrial facilities close to utilizing the detainees as slave work. Both Primo Levi and Nobel Prize victor Elie Wiesel endured Monowitz's inhumane imprisonment.

At the point when Auschwitz was captured, it had more than 40 camps and subcamps.

How did Auschwitz work?

From everywhere, Europeans were packed into railroad cars without windows, latrines, seats, or food, and moved to Auschwitz.

The last group was requested to strip exposed and gave the boot for "delousing" - doublespeak utilized for the gas chambers.

Gatekeepers from the purported "Sterile Institute" would then drop ground-breaking Zyklon-B gas pellets into the fixed loads and trust that individuals will die. It took around 20 minutes. The thick dividers could not shroud the shouts of those dying inside.

At that point, Sonderkommandos - different detainees, for the most part, Jews compelled to work for the gatekeepers or be murdered - would remove fake appendages, glasses, hair, and teeth before hauling the carcasses to the incinerators. Remains of the bodies were covered or utilized as manure.

The Last Solution

The root of the "Last Solution," the Nazi plan to eradicate the Jewish public, stays unsure. What is clear is that the destruction of the Jews was the zenith of a Nazi strategy, under the standard of Adolf Hitler. The "Last Solution" was actualized in stages.

After the Nazi Party took control, state-implemented prejudice brought about the enemy of Jewish enactment, blacklists, "Aryanization," and, lastly, the "Evening of Broken Glass" slaughter, all of which expected to eliminate the Jews from German culture. After World War II, anti-Jewish strategy advanced into a thorough arrangement to think and, in the long run, destroy European Jewry.

The Nazis set up ghettos invaded Poland. Clean and western European Jews were in front of these ghettos. During Germany's attack on the Soviet Union in 1941, portable murdering crews (Einsatzgruppen) started slaughtering the whole Jewish people. The strategies utilized, principally shooting or gas vans, were before long viewed as wasteful and as a mental weight on the executioners.

After the Wannsee Conference in January 1942, the Nazis started the precise removal of Jews from everywhere in Europe to six elimination camps built up in a previous

Polish area - Chelmno, Belzec, Sobibor, Treblinka, Auschwitz-Birkenau, and Majdanek. Elimination camps were murdering focuses intended to complete decimation. Around 3,000,000 Jews were gassed in annihilation camps.

Ultimately, the "Last Solution" (View This Term in the Glossary) comprised of gassings, shootings, arbitrary demonstrations of fear, sickness, and starvation that represented the passings of around 6,000,000 Jews—66% of European Jewry.

Key Dates

June 22, 1941:

Murdering crews go with the German attack of the Soviet Union. German versatile executing crews, called outstanding obligation units (Einsatzgruppen), are relegated to slaughter Jews during the invasion of the Soviet Union. These crews follow the German armed force as it travels far into the Soviet region and commits mass-murder. From the start, the versatile executing crews shoot Jewish men principally. Before long, any place the slaughtering crews go, they shoot every Jewish man, woman, and youngster, without respect for age or sexual orientation. By the spring of 1943, the portable executing crews will have murdered more than a million Jews and countless sectarians, Roma (Gypsies), and Soviet political authorities.

December 8, 1941:

The first executing community starts activity. The Chelmno executing focus starts activity. The Nazis later build up to five other such camps: Belzec, Sobibor, Treblinka, Auschwitz-Birkenau (part of the Auschwitz complex), and Majdanek. At Chelmno, casualties are in gas vans (airtight fixed trucks with motor fumes pumped to the inside compartments). The Belzec, Sobibor, and Treblinka camps use carbon monoxide gas produced by fixed motors joined to gas chambers. Auschwitz-Birkenau, the biggest of the murdering camps, has four substantial gas chambers utilizing Zyklon-B (View This Term in the Glossary) (glasslike hydrogen cyanide) executing specialist. The gas chambers at Majdanek utilize both carbon monoxide and Zyklon-B. (View This Term in the Glossary) Millions of Jews are executed in the gas chambers in the murdering camps as a significant aspect of the "Last Solution."

January 20, 1942:

Wannsee Conference and the "Last Solution". The Wannsee Conference, a gathering between the SS (the first-class watchmen of the Nazi state) and German government offices, opens in Berlin. They talk about and facilitate the execution of the "Last Solution," which is now underway. At Wannsee, the S.S. assesses that the "Last Solution" (View This Term in the Glossary) will include 11 million European Jews, including those from non-occupied nations, like Ireland, Sweden, Turkey, and

Great Britain. Between the fall of 1941 and 1944, the German railroads transport many individuals to their deaths in executing focuses in occupied Poland.

With the steady ascent of the troublesome manner of speaking in the U.S. and Europe, it is essential to recollect how overlooking differing voices can add to the moral decay inside a culture. For example, a few center Jewish qualities apply to medication, remembering an concentration on the conservation of life. By mid-1933, Germany's expert clinical network exiled Jews from their positions through work segregation followed by blame, going before significant Nazi lawful decrees. Professional establishments surrendered their obligations to the individual patient for a cultural concentration on monetary worth and eugenic cleanliness, which, as late grants have appeared, even got arranged into proficient morals educational programs for German clinical students. This fixation on racial-public personality virtue swelled into a mainly clinical type of destruction. While the acceleration was because of numerous perplexing elements past the extent of a solitary paper, the underlying ethnocentric-based rejection of voices from amazing proficient organizations added to thedebasement of social mores. We place that proficient separation served not just like a stage in the developing abuse of Jews explicitly, yet also as a method for overlooking social lessons which would have opposed proficient traps in Nazi needs more by and large.

We balance Jewish lessons with a recorded audit of Third Reich medication, specifically the T-4 killing system's advancement, as a philosophical contextual investigation in different lessons. This recorded model delineates how the clinical calling can neglect to serve and secure minimized gatherings, to a limited extent, by whether the calling has decided to incorporate those persecuted voices inside itself as a method for self-scrutinizing. We will examine six centralJewish qualities—life, harmony, equity, kindness, grant, and genuineness of aim—which could have motivated medical care experts to shield minorities had these guiding principles not been disregarded or mutilated by the modelers of the Third Reich medication. These standards draw on the Jewish group of Written and Oral Torah, just as later compelling Jewish works tended to explicitly identify doctors as experts. These lessons more than once underline the natural expert duty of doctors toward their patients in settling on choices about existence, wellbeing, and at last, passing. These honest mistakes and extreme disappointments of the Third Reich depend on this principal interruption of the patient-doctor relationship and the debasement of patient-focused clinical demonstrable skills.

Advanced doctors may not appreciate the broad job doctors performed during the cultural acceleration of destruction under the Third Reich. Although the Nuremberg Doctors' Trial enlightened a subset of the most grievous behaviors, (pp17–18), the medicalization and maintainability of the sanitization and destructive practices needed the foundational help of the clinical network.

Chapter Six
Second World War

In 1939, there were around 2 billion people on the planet. The best gauges demonstrate that somewhere in the range of 62 and 78 million of them would perish due to WWII— over 3% of the total populace. While prior wars likewise brought about civilians' passings, five regular people were especially intensely influenced by WWII with about a portion of the WWII European setbacks being regular people. Somewhere in the range of 9.8 and 10.4 million regular people were killed for political or racial reasons by the Nazi system (Auerbach, 1992). Deaths because of the war were inconsistent across nations, regardless of whether they were military passings because of battle, regular citizen passings, or the Holocaust – the division of the 1939 populace who passed on in a massive exhibit of influenced nations. Among European nations, Germany and Poland endured the worst part of these losses. Conversely and for similar purposes, American causalities in the European and Asian theaters consolidated were somewhat more than 400,000, the greater part of whom were officers—likewise, all-out deaths in the U.K.

Generally, men died during the war, creating low male/female proportions in Europe after the war, just as numerous dads' absence during the respondents' youth years. Since the male inclination in deaths concentrated among troopers as a regular citizen and holocaust fatalities were, to a great extent, unbiased. With 3 million military deaths, the most affected nation in our information was Germany.

One prompt result of the war by nation and period was the part of people who had their father missing when they were ten years of age. The most significant impacts occurred in the war-attacked nations of Austria, Germany, and Poland. In Austria and Germany, around one out of four youngsters lived without their biological dads when they were age ten during the war. Years after the war, the heritage endures since numerous men from 1950–1955 had fathers who died. In Germany, just about 33% of those aged 10 in these years were not living with their biological dad. Missing dad rates fall firmly in the world after the war. We watch war spikes in different nations (Italy, France, Denmark, and Belgium), yet the differentiation with the pre-and post-war years are not as emotional.

One channel by which WWII may have influenced grown-up wellbeing and SES results is hunger. World War II caused a few severe appetite emergencies, which prompted numerous setbacks and may have had long haul impacts on survivors' strength. For instance, since the start of the German occupation in Poland, the circumstance of the non-German populace was poor. The standard caloric admission for the Polish populace was around 930 calories in 1941. The circumstance was most noticeably awful in the Warsaw Ghetto, where normal food proportions were around 186 calories for each day in 1941.

Thus, in the fall and winter of 1941 1942, Greece was struck by severe starvation with around 100,000 to 200,000 deaths (Hionidou, 2006). In WWII, Greece was under Bulgarian, German, and Italian occupation. The starvation was, for the most part, brought about by three components:

1. Occupiers forced a maritime ban.
2. Costs to ranchers were at such low levels that they were not ready to advertise their items.
3. There was versatility between various districts of the nation that diminished because of occupation.

The wholesome circumstance got back to worthy levels towards the end of 1942. Neelson and Stratman (2011) use Cohort Data to show that the undernourishment of youngsters who were 1 or 2 years of age at that time had an altogether lower likelihood.

A blend of a food barricade and a brutal winter prompted a serious appetite emergency in winter 1944/1945 in the Netherlands. Around 20,000 deaths, fundamentally among older men, are credited to this starvation. The starvation finished with the end of the German occupation in May 1945. A generally supported populace influenced the Dutch starvation at a quiet time and area. People presented to this starvation in utero are shown to experience the ill effects of psychological and mental issues, and fixation, diabetes, and coronary illness, and they additionally perform worse concerning anthropometric and financial markers.

Germany experienced hunger somewhere in 1945 and 1948 when the food from occupied nations stopped. In the U.S. occupation zone, the Office of Military Government for Germany built up an objective of 1550 calories every day in 1945. However, in the principal long stretches of occupation, this objective regularly could not be met. There were locales where regular calories every day were around 700 (Gimbel, 1968). Death rates were raised by factor 4 for grown-ups and 10 for babies during this period. With a decent collection and cash change in June 1948, nutritional deficiencies were survived (Zink, 1957).

In World War II in Europe, Germany looked to maintain a strategic distance from a long war. Germany's technique was to overcome its rivals in a progression of short missions. Germany rapidly overran quite a bit of Europe and was successful for over two years by depending on another military strategy called the "Raid" or "Blitzkrieg" (lightning war). Quick assault strategies required the centralization of hostile weapons (tanks, planes, and ordnance) along a restricted front. These powers would drive a break in enemy safeguards, allowing heavily armored tank divisions to infiltrate quickly and wander unreservedly behind adversary lines, causing stun and confusion among the opponent's protections. German air power kept the opponent from enough resupplying or redeploying powers, and in this way, sending fortifications to seal holes in the front.

Germany victories (1939/1942)

- Poland (assaulted in September 1939)
- Denmark (April 1940)
- Norway (April 1940)
- Belgium (May 1940)
- Netherlands (May 1940)
- Luxembourg (May 1940)
- France (May 1940)
- Yugoslavia (April 1941)
- Greece (April 1941)

Germany did not defeat Great Britain, which was shielded from German assault by the English Channel, Royal Navy and Royal Air Force (Raf)

On June 22, 1941, German powers out of nowhere attacked the Soviet Union. However, Germany was unable to vanquish the Soviet Union, which along with Great Britain and the United States, reversed the fight and crushed Germany in May 1945.

Notwithstanding the proceeding war with Great Britain, German powers attacked the Soviet Union in June 1941. From the start, the German Blitzkrieg appeared to succeed. Soviet powers were driven back more than 600 miles to the doors of Moscow, with great misfortunes. In December 1941, Hitler singularly proclaimed war on the United States, which therefore included its colossal monetary and military capacity to the alliance showed against him. A second German attack against the Soviet Union in 1942 reached the shores of the Volga River and the city of Stalingrad. Nonetheless, the Soviet Union dispatched a counteroffensive in November 1942, catching and annihilating a whole German armed force at Stalingrad.

Germany was incapable of vanquishing the Soviet Union, which, along with Great Britain and the United States, reversed Germany's activity. Germany got entangled in a long war, leading at last to its thrashing in May 1945.

Raid strategies unquestionably had an enormous influence in the thrashing of Germany's foes. The Germans unquestionably had prevalent airpower with their Ju-87 Stuka jump aircraft. The Luftwaffe governed the skies with a larger part in numbers and a more powerful airplane. On the ground, in any case, it was a different issue. The British and French tanks dwarfed the Panzers (German tanks). The strategy made them unrivaled. The British and French spread their tanks out. They gave every infantry company a specific number of tanks. Perhaps a couple, possibly a couple of more, the fundamental message is that their tanks were pretty much autonomous and battled close by infantry. The distinction with the German tanks was that they moved into divisions. They had Panzer heavily armored divisions of around 300 or 400 tanks, which were substantially more remarkable than an infantry area with a couple of tanks. The massing of tanks was likewise a piece of Blitzkrieg, and that helped tremendously. The object of shock assumed a significant part in the war. Poland had a vast number of men, and if they realized the Germans were coming, Germany actually would have won, however they would have endured significantly more significant losses.

Raid was a brilliant war strategy, yet it was not the primary explanation behind which Germany vanquished its adversaries. Additionally, Germany was thoughtfully new to assault and knew the territories where they would not be required to come through.

The Maginot Line was a progression of substantial powers along the French-German fringe. It was 93 miles in length, yet it was 250 miles shy of the ocean. The French started assembling expansions; however, they could not do so in time. The French had 400,000 men on the Maginot Line, and both the French and the Germans realized that assaulting the Maginot line would be self-destructive. The Allies anticipated that the Germans would assault from northern Belgium. They thought this because southern Belgium was home to the Ardennes, a sloping area canvassed in woodland. The Allies anticipated that the Germans assaulted from that point if, and a major IF at that point would take those fourteen days.

However, to get through the thick woods and all said and done uniquely in little numbers. The Germans assaulted from that point, and the French just had 100,000 unequipped, gravely prepared men. The Germans got through the slopes in 3 days, and through others by many thousands, 1800 Panzers got through, and infantry segments came through by the thousands.

They entered France and caught the Allied soldiers in Belgium. The way that they overcame in 3 days assumed a significant job. The result would have been distinctive as the 500,000 soldiers up north could have returned to help if it had taken them longer. The advancement was on account of German military architects, street developers, and destruction crews. They exploded trees, lay streets, and cleared courses through to permit the Germans to get past. It was another strategy utilized other than Blitzkrieg to enable the Germans to decimate their foes. Hitler's sheer virtuoso helped the circumstance a ton. He utilized his military's primary flood to hover around and trap the 500,000 partnered troops in Belgium. The primary wave caught them there as the remainder of the German soldiers attacked France. They traveled 200 miles in 7 days, and very soon, 12,000,000 outcasts were clogging France's roads. The Luftwaffe made arbitrary goes at the exiles killing; however, many as would be prudent. The way that the French government and military pioneers changed around then did not help. The Commander in Chief was Gamelin.

He was cunning; however, he had no guts. Also, he was 62. He seldom walked outside of the French central command at Vincennes (which did not have any radio interchanges which could not make the circumstance any better). He was somewhat old for the job. The Premier got held by Marshal Petain, who was 83. Holland was assaulted, and they were decimated. They gave up on May

14, and Belgium gave up on May 27. May 25, Bologne fell, on the 26th Calais. Hitler had won. Dunkirk lost on June 4, and the Allies got back wounded and battered. The English grabbed any vessels that they could find and sent them in to clear the poor soldiers. Hitler portrayed the clash of Dunkirk as one of the best German triumphs of all time. Germans were celebrating on that night.

Mussolini joined the war as Hitler's partner on June 10. He was reasonably useful to Hitler as he had some of Northern Africa and Greece under his control. However, the Allies moved in and moved through the Italian powers very fast. Hitler went to his Italian ally's aid and battled the Allies away by utilizing paratroopers (the first occasion when they were ever utilized adequately). Hitler took the land in a couple of weeks. He did not have the foggiest idea about this at that point; however, his transition to help Mussolini demonstrated deadly to his fundamental objective, the taking of Russia. If he had moved in on Russia only half a month earlier (how long it took to support Mussolini) at that point, today is believed that he may have beaten Russia. It was not the Russian armed force that decimated the Germans. It was the Russian winter. Hitler's taking over of his adversaries was not a direct result of Blitzkrieg (even though it assumed a significant job) yet additionally due to Hitler's sheer genius.

He persuaded Germans to crush their foes by discourse, which he was outward, an extraordinary speaker. What was within in any case, lamentably for the resistance, was a genius. He could carefully put his soldiers to make an almost relentless force. France, Belgium, Holland, Poland, and the entirety of different nations he spread his carnage through, endured incredible misfortunes and were cruelly pounded.

Even though the long early stretches of the decade saw a troublesome money related circumstance because of the Great Depression, Deutsche Luft Hansa further extended its global course network in South America and dispatched booked departures from Germany to the Middle East. Strategically, the organization heads led to the rising Nazi Party; an airplane was made accessible to Adolf Hitler for his mission for the 1932 presidential political election liberated from any charge. Erhard Milch, who had filled in as the head of the aircraft company since 1926, turned into a high-positioning authority at the Aviation Ministry when Hitler took control in 1933.

An essential enthusiasm of Deutsche Luft Hansa around then was the decrease of mail conveyance times. In 1930, the Eurasia Corporation was set up as a joint-venture with the Chinese vehicle service, conceding Luft Hansa a syndication position for mail transport among Germany and China, just as admittance to the Chinese market. To this end, the Shanghai-Nanjing-Beijing course began in the next year utilizing Junkers W 34 sent there. A record was set in 1930 when Vienna's mail course to Istanbul (with visits in Budapest, Belgrade, and Sofia) finished in just 24 hours. By examination, the main transoceanic traveler trip by the aircraft (from Warnemünde to New York City utilizing a Dornier Wal flying vessel) took around a multiweek.

Following a lot of testing, a booked postal course was introduced, between Europe and South America, in 1934. It was the central typically booked carrier administration over a sea on the planet. Wal flying vessels were in use - sling dispatched for the overseas leg. These were brought by the Dornier Do 18 of every 1936 creation activities in non-visual conditions conceivable. The European organization saw the Junkers G.38 (around then the biggest traveler airplane on the planet) on the Berlin-London course utilizing Amsterdam, just as the Junkers Ju 52/3m and Heinkel He 70, which took into account quicker air travel. Its advances were supported "Barrage Services" (German: Blitzstrecken) between Berlin, Hamburg, Cologne, and Frankfurt. In 1935, the primary airplane not made in Germany got into the Luft Hansa armada: two Boeing 247s and one Douglas DC-2.

With the start of the war on September 1, 1939, all regular citizen flight activities of Luft Hansa stopped, and the airplane armada went under an order of the Luftwaffe, alongside most staff. The organization zeroed in on airplane support and repair. Like most of Germany's endeavors during the war, they relied upon constrained work; they stepped up and obtained its own constrained workers from the workshops situated close to the front lines. There were as yet planned traveler trips inside Germany and uninvolved or unbiased nations, yet appointments were confined and served the fighting requests. During the later long periods of the war, most traveler airplanes changed to military vessels.

The Luft Hansa co-activities in foreign nations destroyed: Deruluft stopped was closed down after mediation by the Chinese government. Syndicate Condor nationalized and renamed Cruzeiro do Sul in 1943, trying to delete its German roots.

The last booked trip of Deutsche Luft Hansa – from Berlin to Munich occurred on April 21, 1945, yet the airplane crashed in a matter of seconds before the arranged appearance. Another (non-booked) flight was played out the following day, from Berlin to Warnemünde, which denoted flight activities. Following Germany's surrender and the resulting Allied control of Germany, all airplanes in the nation were seized, and Deutsche Luft Hansa was dissolved. The rest of the benefits were exchanged on January 1, 1951.

On January 31, 1917, Germany reported the recharging of unlimited submarine fighting in the Atlantic as German torpedo-furnished submarines plan to assault any boats, including regular citizen traveler transporters, supposed to be located in combat area waters.

When World War I started in 1914, President Woodrow Wilson promised nonpartisanship for the United States, which most Americans supported. Notwithstanding, England was one of America's nearest trading partners, and strain before long emerged between the United States and Germany over their endeavored barricade of the

British Isles. A few U.S. ships heading out to Britain were sunk by German mines, and, in February 1915, Germany declared unlimited fighting against all boats, impartial or something else, that entered the combat area around Britain. After one month, Germany reported that a German cruiser had sunk the William P. Frye, a private American trader vessel moving grain to England when it vanished. President Wilson was offended, yet the German government apologized, considering the assault a grievous misstep.

The Germans' most considerable maritime weapon was the U-vessel, a submarine unquestionably more advanced than those used by different countries at that point. For a long time, the normal U-pontoon was 214 feet, conveyed 35 men and 12 torpedoes, and could travel submerged for two continuous hours. In the initial days of World War I, the U-vessels negatively affected allied transportation.

Toward the beginning of May 1915, a few New York papers distributed an admonition by the German embassy in Washington that Americans going on British or Allied boats in combat areas did as such at their own risk. The declaration was at the same time as an ad for the unavoidable cruising of the British-claimed Lusitania sea liner from New York to Liverpool. On May 7, the Lusitania was destroyed without notice entirely off the bank of Ireland. Of the 1,959 travelers, 1,198 were murdered, including 128 Americans.

On February 22, Congress passed a $250 million arms-appointments charge planned to prepare the United States for war. After two days, British agents gave the U.S. envoy to Britain a duplicate of what has become known as the "Zimmermann Note," a coded message from German Foreign Secretary Arthur Zimmermann to Count Johann von Bernstorff, the German representative to Mexico. In the wire, captured and translated by the British, Zimmermann expressed that, in case of war with the United States, Mexico ought to be approached to enter the war as a German partner. Consequently, Germany would vow to reestablish Mexico, Texas's lost domains, New Mexico, and Arizona.

Clinical students of history have as of late distributed records that show medical specialists were, in reality, complicit with the Nazis—and became casualties if they were named non-Aryan. Fangerau talked about discoveries with Corinna Hartmann and Andreas Jahn of Gehirn & Geist, the brain science and neuroscience strength publication of Spektrum der Wissenschaft, and the German sister publication of Scientific American.

An altered record of the meeting follows

Educator Fangerau, an examination venture, analyzes the pretended by nervous system specialists during the Nazi time frame. For what reason is this just a brief time afterward?

There were a few distinct stages where individuals managed National Socialism after World War II. Following 1945 the Allies sought after a strategy of denazification. After that, German culture, in general, endeavored to stifle its past. Numerous individuals from the people to come, notwithstanding, thought it was difficult to close their eyes: Students in 1968 were furious that their folks were reluctant to manage the Third Reich. The clinical strengths took much longer to start working through the past. Thus, their reappraisal of the wrongdoings submitted started distinctly during the 1980s.

Part of the motivation behind why recorded examination into nervous system science has just been directed efficiently in recent years is that nervous system science and psychiatry were merged into a similar disciplinary structure in 1935. Before then, nervous system science had started to isolate from psychiatry. The fundamental thought was to leave mental marvels that are hard to comprehend to the specialists and focus on problems that are anatomically self-evident. The National Socialists invalidated this exertion. They accepted that they could control these clinical strengths all the more viably if they united them in the Society of German Neurologists and Psychiatrists, which was overwhelmed by therapists focused on the belief system of racial cleanliness. The administrator of the general public was Ernst Rüdin, a therapist. Thus, nervous system science has come to be as less ensnared. Since the late 1980s, a verifiable examination paints an altogether different picture.

Nervous system science as control was, for sure, complicit in the wrongdoings of the Nazis. The philosophy of racial cleanliness joined with sharp contentions about sympathy and cost decreases served to legitimize the deliberate executing of more than 70,000 disabled individuals. The Nazis metaphorically called this strategy killing. The two nervous system specialists and therapists were included, and it is regularly hard to recognize who was a nervous system specialist and who was a specialist. The specialists surveyed patients, and whomever they discovered to be either risky or unequipped for working was moved to an executing office and killed. Neuroscientists, at that point, utilized the cerebrums of these dead patients in their exploration.

Hallervorden directed "auxiliary examination" for the willful extermination program on the slaughtered patients' ailments as the top of the histopathology division. In addition to other things, he and his colleagues contemplated which neurological and mental sicknesses are inherited. These conclusions shaped the reason for the choice of patients to be murdered. The Kaiser Wilhelm

Institute got vast quantities of cerebrums of killing casualties for its examination. Furthermore, as we presently know, the individuals who partook in that examination were very aware of their root.

Unscrupulous clinical experimentation (without tolerant assent or any shields) completed during the Third Reich is divided into three classifications.

1. Trials managing the endurance of military staff

Numerous trials in the camps planned to encourage the endurance of Axis military faculty in the field. For instance, at Dachau, doctors from the German flying corps and the German Experimental Institution for Aviation led high-elevation probes detainees to decide the most significant height from which groups of a disabled airplane could parachute to security. Researchers there additionally completed supposed freezing probes of detainees to locate a powerful treatment for hypothermia. Detainees were likewise used to test different strategies for making seawater drinkable.

2. Analyses to test medications and medicines

Different analyses created and tested medications and treatment strategies for wounds and ailments, which

German military and occupation forces experienced in the field. Researchers utilized camp prisoners to test vaccination mixes and antibodies for the anticipation at the inhumane German imprisonments of Sachsenhausen, Dachau, Natzweiler, Buchenwald, and Neuengamme. Prisoners were also used for treatment of infectious illnesses, including intestinal sickness, typhus, tuberculosis, typhoid fever, yellow fever, and irresistible hepatitis. Doctors at Ravensbrück directed investigations in bone-joining and tried recently created sulfa (sulfanilamide) drugs. At Natzweiler and Sachsenhausen, detainees were presented to phosgene and mustard gas to test potential remedies.

3. Analyses to propel Nazi racial and philosophical objectives:

The third classification of clinical experimentation tried to propel the racial and philosophical fundamentals of the Nazi perspective. The most notorious was the investigations of Josef Mengele on twins of any age at Auschwitz. He likewise coordinated investigations on Roma (Gypsies), as did Werner Fischer at Sachsenhausen, to decide how extraordinary "races" withstood different infectious illnesses. The exploration of August Hirt at Strasbourg University likewise proposed to set up "Jewish racial mediocrity." Additional grisly analyses intended to encourage Nazi racial objectives incorporated a progression of sanitization (View This Term in the Glossary) tests attempted basically at Auschwitz and

Ravensbrück. Researchers tried various techniques with an end goal to build up a proficient and cheap methodology for the mass disinfection.

The Nuremberg Code

The Nuremberg Code was made in the outcome of the revelation of the camp analyses and resulting preliminaries to address submitted by clinical experts during the Holocaust. The Nuremberg Code incorporated the guideline of educated assent and required principles for research.

Chapter Seven

The events that followed?

After the significant Allied invasion of western France, Germany accumulated hold powers and dispatched a huge counter force in the Ardennes, which had fallen by January. Simultaneously, Soviet powers were moving in from the east, attacking Poland and East Prussia. By March, Western Allied powers were crossing the Rhine River, catching countless soldiers from Germany's Army Group B. The Red Army had in the interim entered Austria, and the two fronts immediately moved toward Berlin. Critical besieging efforts by Allied airplanes were beating A German area, once in a while pulverizing whole urban communities in a night. In early 1945, Germany set up a furious guard, however quickly lost domain, ran out of provisions, and depleted its choices. In April, Allied powers pushed through the German guarded line in Italy. East met West on the River Elbe on April 25, 1945, when Soviet and American soldiers met near Torgau, Germany. At that point came the Third Reich's finish, as the Soviets took Berlin, Adolf Hitler ended it all on April 30, and Germany gave up unequivocally on all fronts on May 8 (May 7 on the Western Front). Hitler's "Thousand-Year Reich" lasted just 12 amazingly ruinous years.

No big surprise. It was not only the Second World War; it was a war to the subsequent force, exponentially more terrible. Not merely in degree and amount—in loss of life and geographic reach—yet also in results, if one thought about Auschwitz and Hiroshima.

In any case, in 1960, there were two remarkable turns of events, two catches: In May, Israeli agents captured Adolf Eichmann in Argentina and flew him to Jerusalem for trial. In October, William L. Shirer caught something different, both monstrous and slippery, in The Third Reich's rise and fall. He caught it such that made amnesia not, at this point, a choice. Another version of the 50th anniversary of the book's publication, the National Book Award, reviews a significant purpose of expression in American chronicled cognizance.

The capture of Eichmann, a working head officer of the Final Solution, stirred the question Why? Why had Germany, who exceptionally taught social orders on earth, changed itself into an instrument that transformed a landmass into a charnel house? Why had Germany given itself over to the raving exterminations directives of one man, the man Shirer alludes to derisively as a "drifter"? For what reason did the world permit a "tramp," a Chaplinesque figure whose 1923 brew hall putsch was a comic disaster, to turn into a destructive Führer whose standard spread over the mainland and took steps to last a thousand years?

History is not fate, and we ought to be wary about going too far in drawing comparisons with the past. The past is, as L.P. Hartley put it, a foreign nation. However, would we be able to learn anything from the radicalism of the 1930s?

All the more explicitly, would we be able to see how fanatic gatherings rose and what sort of individuals became leaders?

Understanding what spurred a colossal number of ordinary Germans to help the Nazi party (NSDAP) has been the objective of historians and political researchers for quite a long time. Studies that feature their ubiquity among certain social classes are likely the most revered and diligent. What is more, the humanist Seymour Lipset was among the first to portray the ordinary Nazi citizen in 1932 as:

"A working-class independently employed Protestant who lived either on a homestead or in a little network and who had recently decided in favor of an anti-extremist or regionalist ideological group firmly contradicted the force and impact of large business and enormous work."

Others, for example, an American student of history, William Burstein, have attempted to uphold for the Nazi party by featuring personal financial circumstances. People whose material interests lined up with the group's foundation would be bound to become individuals.

In any case, different examinations contend that the Nazis drew from the less fortunate in the public eye or had a mass allure over the political range. Maybe the leading gathering for which there is an agreement concerning help for the Nazis is Catholics: reliably, Catholics seem to have been more averse to decide in favor of the NSDAP or to become members of the Party. Things being what they are, who precisely were the Nazis?

Ascending the stepping stool

Many have returned to this old inquiry with new and more definite information. They inspected a unique dataset of around 10,000 World War II German fighters from the 1930s and 1940s, which contains actual data on social foundation, such as occupation and instruction, just as different qualities, such as religion, criminal record, and military help.

It is said that the individuals from Nazi associations – regardless of whether they were early joiners who joined during the 1920s or the individuals who joined during the 1940s – were bound to originate from high-status foundations and had more significant levels of education, with individuals from a higher-status foundation twice as liable to join the Nazi party as somebody from a lower-status foundation. We additionally affirmed that Catholics were more averse to be part of Nazi associations.

Such itemized information permits us to delve further into the foundations of Nazi individuals.

True to form, Nazi members seemed to have progressed farther than non-members, for instance, climbing from occupations sorted as "talented, a tailor to a semi-proficient work, for example, educator. What is generally excellent, in any case, is that this headway does not seem to have been driven by the get-together compensating its individuals with higher-status positions.

By looking at the jobs that these people prepared for at an early stage in their vocations, and not merely their expressed occupations, we locate that early developments drove people to ascend the social stepping stool – Nazi associations appear to have pulled in upwardly mobile people.

In reality, this appears to have been the case for the Nazi party itself, including the S.S., S.A., and Hitler Youth. These were individuals who were at that point, advancing throughout everyday life. Even though we cannot state from the information whether individuals profited in different manners, such as direct budgetary prizes or non-money related advantages, the more prominent social progression of Nazi individuals that we do watch does not seem to have been driven only by enrollment.

What does this all mean for the overall comprehension of the kind of individuals that joined Nazi associations? While it is challenging to reveal what inspired individuals to join the Nazis, our discoveries propose that many educated and eager individuals from the higher levels of the social scale were included.

The examination causes to see how the Nazi party rose and came to control long before WWII yet, also gives us a knowledge into how radical associations can shape and pull in individuals all the more by and large. It shows that the past has an unadulterated philosophy regarding inspirations for joining radical gatherings and looking at financial and social factors.

Toward the end of World War II, enormous areas of Europe and Asia were in ruins. Suburbs were redrawn, and homecomings, ejections, and internments were in progress. However, the gigantic endeavors to revamp had quite recently started. When the war started in the late 1930s, the total population was around 2 billion. In under ten years, the war between the Axis the Allied forces had brought about 80 million deaths - slaughtering around 4 percent of the entire world population. United powers currently became occupiers, assuming responsibility for Germany, Japan, and a significant part of the region they had dominated. Endeavors were made to forever destroy those countries' war-production capacities, as processing plants were demolished, and the previous initiative was eliminated or arraigned. Atrocities occurred in Europe and Asia, prompting numerous executions and jail sentences. A considerable number of Germans and Japanese were coercively removed from places they called home. Associated occupations and United Nations choices created some dependable issues later on, including the strains that made East and West Germany. Also created were unique plans on the Korean Peninsula that prompted North and South Korea production and - the Korean War in 1950. The United Nations Plan for Palestine made Israel proclaim its freedom in 1948 and started the Arab-Israeli clash. The developing strains between Western forces and the Soviet Eastern Bloc became the Cold War, and the turn of events and multiplication of atomic weapons raised the genuine possibility of an inconceivable World War III if the shared conviction could not be found. World War II was the most incredible story of the twentieth century, and its result keeps on influencing the world significantly over 65 years after the fact.

During World War II, the Nazis expelled somewhere between 7,000,000 and 9,000,000 Europeans, generally to Germany. Inside months of Germany's surrender in May 1945, the Allies sent back to their nations of origin more than 6,000,000 uprooted people (D.P.s; wartime exiles). Between 1.5 million and 2 million DPs denied bringing home.

Most Jewish survivors, who had to endure inhumane imprisonments or had been secluded from everything, could not or were reluctant to return to Eastern Europe due to after-war discrimination against Jews and their networks' annihilation during the Holocaust. Vast numbers of the individuals who returned dreaded for their lives. In Poland, for instance, local people started a few fierce slaughters. The most exceedingly awful was the one in Kielce in 1946 in which 42 Jews, all survivors of the Holocaust, were slaughtered. This slaughter prompted a critical second development of Jewish outcasts from Poland toward the West.

Numerous Holocaust survivors moved toward the West to regions freed by the western Allies. They were housed in uprooted people (D.P.) camps and metropolitan areas for displaced people. The Allies built up such camps in Allied-occupied Germany, Austria, and Italy for outcasts standing by to leave Europe. The vast majority of the Jewish uprooted people were in the British occupation zone in northern Germany and the American southern occupation zone. The British set up an enormous dislodged people camp contiguous to Bergen-Belsen in Germany. A few vast camps holding 4,000 to 6,000 displaced people each—Feldafing, Landsberg, and Foehrenwald—were situated in the American zone.

At its top is 1947, the Jewish uprooted individual population came to around 250,000. An assortment of Jewish organizations was dynamic in the uprooted people camps.

The American Jewish Joint Distribution Committee furnished displaced people with food and apparel, and the Organization for Rehabilitation through Training (ORT) offered professional preparation. Jewish dislodged people additionally started self-administering associations, and many moved in the direction of the foundation of a Jewish state in Palestine. There were boards of Jewish uprooted people in the American and British zones, which, as their essential objectives, squeezed for more prominent migration openings and the foundation of a Jewish country in Palestine.

In the United States, movement limitations greatly restricted the number of exiles allowed to enter the nation. The British, who had gotten a command from the League of Nations to regulate Palestine, incredibly reduced Jewish migration there to a great extent on Arab complaints. Numerous nations shut their borders to movement. Notwithstanding these obstructions, numerous Jewish dislodged people endeavored to leave Europe as quickly as time permitted.

The Jewish Brigade Group, started as a unit inside the British armed force in late 1944, worked with previous sectarians to help sort out the Brihah (actually "escape"), the departure of 250,000 Jewish displaced people across shut borders from inside Europe to the coast trying to cruise for Palestine. The Mossad le-Aliyah Bet, an organization built up by Palestine's Jewish authority, composed "unlawful" movement (Aliyah Bet) by transport. Notwithstanding, the British captured the vast majority of the boats.

In 1947, for instance, the British halted the Exodus 1947 at the port of Haifa. The boat had 4,500 Holocaust survivors ready, who was sent back to Germany on British vessels. By and large, the British confined the evacuees—more than 50,000—in detainment camps on Cyprus in the eastern Mediterranean Sea. The British utilization of confinement camps as an impediment fizzled, and the surge of outsiders entering into Palestine proceeded.

Chapter Eight

Conclusion

After the war, the top enduring German pioneers pursued Nazi Germany's wrongdoings, including the Holocaust violations. Their preliminary was before an International Military Tribunal (IMT) in Nuremberg, Germany. Judges from the Allied forces—Great Britain, France, the Soviet Union, and the United States—managed about 22 significant Nazi hoodlums. Hence, the United States held 12 extra trials in Nuremberg of significant level authorities of the German government, military, and S.S. just as clinical experts and driving industrialists. The violations charged under the Nuremberg courts' watchful eye were wrongdoings against harmony, atrocities, violations against humankind, and intrigue to perpetrate any prior violations.

On the whole, 199 litigants were tried at Nuremberg, and 161 were indicted, whereas 37 were condemned to death, including 12 of those tried by the IMT. Holocaust violations were included for a couple of the trials but were the significant focal point of just the U.S. preliminary Einsatzgruppen pioneers. The litigants, by and large, recognized that the wrongdoings they were blamed for happened, however rejected that they were responsible, as they were following orders from higher authority.

The Nazis' most extraordinary power, the individual most at fault for the Holocaust, was absent at the trials. Adolf

Hitler had killed himself in the last days of the war, as had a few of his nearest associates. Some fled Germany to live abroad, including hundreds who went to the United States.

Trials of the Nazis continued both in Germany and in numerous other nations. Simon Wiesenthal, a Nazi-tracker, assisted atrocities examiners about Adolf Eichmann. Eichmann, who had helped plan and completed many Jews' extraditions, was brought to Israel. The declaration of several observers, a significant number of the survivors, was followed everywhere worldwide. Eichmann was convicted and executed in 1962

Key Dates

August 8, 1945

Sanction of the International Military Tribunal (IMT) was declared at London Conference.

The International Military Tribunal (IMT) was made out of judges from the United States, Great Britain, France, and the Soviet Union. Driving Nazi authorities will be arraigned and investigated in Nuremberg, Germany, under Article 6 of the IMT's Charter for the accompanying wrongdoings: (1) Conspiracy to carry out charges 2, 3, and 4, which are recorded here; (2) wrongdoings against harmony—characterized as cooperation in the arranging and pursuing of a war of animosity disregarding various worldwide deals; (3) atrocities—characterized as an infringement of the globally settled upon rules for taking

up arms; and (4) violations against humankind—
"specifically, murder, eradication, oppression, removal, and
other obtuse acts carried out against any regular citizen
populace, previously or during the war; or mistreatment on
political, racial, or strict grounds in the execution of or
regarding any wrongdoing inside the ward of the Tribunal,
regardless of whether disregarding homegrown law of the
nation where executed."

October 6, 1945

Driving Nazi authorities arraigned for atrocities.

The four chief investigators of the International Military
Tribunal (IMT)— Robert H. Jackson (United States),
Francois de Menthon (France), Roman A. Rudenko
(Soviet Union), and Sir Hartley Shawcross (Great
Britain)— hand down arraignments against 24 driving
Nazi authorities. The arraigned include Hermann Göring
(Hitler's previous representative), Rudolf Hess (agent
pioneer of the Nazi Party), Joachim von Ribbentrop
(unfamiliar pastor), Wilhelm Keitel (head of the military),
Wilhelm Frick (priest of the inside), Ernst Kaltenbrunner
(head of security powers), Hans Frank (lead representative
general of invaded Poland), Konstantin von Neurath
(legislative leader of Bohemia and Moravia), Erich Raeder
(head of the naval force), Karl Doenitz (Raeder's
replacement), Alfred Jodl (military order), Alfred

Rosenberg (serve for invaded eastern domains), Baldur von Schirach (head of the Hitler Youth), Julius Streicher (extremist Nazi bigoted distributer), Fritz Sauckel (head of constrained work portion), Albert Speer (weapons clergyman), and Arthur Seuss-Inquart (official for the invaded Netherlands). Martin Bormann (Hitler's auxiliary) is to be in absentia.

October 1, 1946
Decision at Nuremberg:

The International Military Tribunal (IMT) declares its decisions. It forces capital punishment on 12 litigants (Göring, Ribbentrop, Keitel, Kaltenbrunner, Rosenberg, Frank, Frick, Streicher, Sauckel, Jodl, Seyss-Inquart, and Bormann). Three were condemned to life detainment (Hess, financial matters head Walther Funk, and Raeder). Four get jail terms extending from 10 to 20 years (Doenitz, Schirach, Speer, and Neurath). The court absolves three respondents: Hjalmar Schacht (financial matters head), Franz von Papen (German legislator who assumed a significant part in Hitler's appointment as chancellor), and Hans Fritzsche (head of press and radio). On October 16, 1946, the capital punishments were done with two exceptional cases: Göring ended his planned execution, and Bormann stayed missing. The other ten litigants hanged, their bodies incinerated, and the remains poured in the Iser River. The seven significant war lawbreakers condemned to jail terms remanded to the Spandau Prison in Berlin.

Prisoners of the camp:

As the Jews were the principal focuses of Nazi annihilation, the executing communities' casualties were overwhelmingly Jewish. In the several constrained work and death camps not outfitted with gassing offices, nonetheless, others from an expansive scope of foundations could likewise be found. Detainees were needed to wear shading coded triangles on their coats to ensure that the camp's watchmen and officials could undoubtedly distinguish every individual's experience and set the various gatherings in opposition to one another. Political detainees, for example, Communists, Socialists, and exchange unionists, wore red triangles. Basic hoodlums sported green. Roma (Gypsies) and others the Germans considered "asocial" or "indolent" wore dark triangles. Jehovah's Witnesses donned purple and gay people pink. Letters demonstrated identity: P represented Polish, S.U. for the Soviet Union, F for French.

Caught Soviet officers functioned as constrained workers, and a large number of these detainees of war died because they were executed or gravely abused by the Germans. On the whole, more than 3,000,000 died on account of the Germans.

Twenty-three thousand German and Austrian Roma (Gypsies) were prisoners of Auschwitz, and around 20,000 were slaughtered there. Romani (Gypsy) men, ladies, and kids were limited together in a different camp. On the evening of August 2, 1944, an enormous gathering of Roma gassed in the demolition of the "Vagabond family camp." Nearly 3,000 Roma were killed, including many of the ladies and youngsters. A portion of the men sent to constrained work camps in Germany, where many died. By and large, countless Roma from everywhere in German-occupied Europe were killed in camps and by versatile executing crews.

Political detainees, Jehovah's Witnesses, and gay people were sent to death camps as a discipline. Individuals from these three groups were not focused, as were Jews and Roma, for precise homicide. In any case, many died in the camps from starvation, illness, weariness, and severe treatment.

July 1, 1937

Martin Niemoeller, nonconformist church pioneer, captured.

Martin Niemoeller, one of the fundamental rivals of the Nazi racial belief system in the Lutheran church and one of the authors of the oppositional "Confession booth Church," is captured. He is sent to the Sachsenhausen inhumane imprisonment in 1938 and goes through seven years in death camps. After the war, Niemoeller's judgment of observers to Nazi approaches will turn into a call to early activity. His words: "First they sought the communists, and I did not stand up — because I was not a communist. At that point, they sought the exchange unionists, and I did not stand up—because I was not an exchange unionist. At that point, they sought the Jews, and I did not stand up—because I was not a Jew. At that point, they sought me—and there was nobody left to represent me."

June 6, 1941

German High Command orders slaughtering of Soviet commissars.

Fourteen days before the German attack on the Soviet Union, the central leadership of the German military issues requests to screen Soviet prisoners of war (POWs) for Soviet commissars. The commissars were given over to the versatile murdering crews (Einsatzgruppen) for guaranteed execution. Between June 22, 1941, and May 9, 1945, over 3,000,000 Soviet prisoners of war died in German authority. Most perish from starvation, sickness, and presentation, albeit several thousand, are shot as Communists, Jews, or "Asiatics."

August 2–3, 1944

"Vagabond camp" at Auschwitz shut.

Twenty-three thousand Roma (Gypsies) were expelled to Auschwitz-Birkenau and set in a different part of the camp. Conditions there were exceedingly terrible. Practically all the Roma in Auschwitz were gassed, worked to death, or casualties of sickness. The Nazis characterize Roma as racially sub-par, and their destiny intently matches that of Jews. On August 2–3, 1944, the "Vagabond camp" at Auschwitz-Birkenau was shut. The remaining Romani (Gypsy) men, ladies, and kids were slaughtered in the gas chambers. Up to 250,000 Roma were killed in the Holocaust.

Close to the war's end, when Germany's military power crumbled, the Allied militaries surrounded the Nazi camps. The Soviets drew nearer from the east and the British, French, and Americans from the West.

The Germans started hysterically to move the detainees out of the camps close to the front and accept them as constrained workers in camps inside Germany. Detainees were first taken via train and afterward by foot on "death walks," as they were known.

Detainees had to walk long distances in unpleasant cold, with next to zero food, water, or rest. The individuals who could not keep up were shot. The most significant death walks occurred in the winter of 1944-1945 when the Soviet armed force started its liberation of Poland. Nine days before the Soviets showed up at Auschwitz, the Germans walked a vast number of detainees out of the camp toward Wodzislaw, a town 35 miles away, where they were put on cargo trains to different camps. Around one out of four died in transit.

The Nazis frequently murdered huge gatherings of detainees previously, during, or after walks. During one walk, 7,000 Jewish detainees, 6,000 of the ladies, were moved from camps in the Danzig locale verged north by the Baltic Sea. On the ten-day walk, 700 were killed. Those still alive when the marchers arrived at the ocean's shores were crashed into the water and shot.

January 18, 1945

Passing walks from the Auschwitz camp framework started.

The S.S. starts clearing Auschwitz and its satellite camps, almost 60,000 detainees are constrained on death walks from the Auschwitz camp framework. Thousands were killed long before the death walk. A considerable number of detainees, generally Jews, are compelled to walk to the city of Wodzislaw in the western Upper Silesia. S.S. watchers shoot any individual who falls behind or cannot continue. More than 15,000 perish during the death walks from Auschwitz. In Wodzislaw, the detainees are put on unheated cargo cars and expelled to death camps in Germany, especially to Flossenbuerg, Sachsenhausen, Gross-Rosen, Buchenwald, Dachau, and Mauthausen. On January 27, 1945, the Soviet armed force entered Auschwitz and freed a couple of residual detainees.

January 25, 1945

The departure and death walk from Stutthof death camp.

The departure of almost 50,000 detainees, the lion's share of the Jews, starts from the Stutthof camp framework in northern Poland. Around 5,000 detainees from Stutthof subcamps are walked to the Baltic Sea coast, constrained into the water, and machine-gunned. Different detainees are put on a passing walk to Lauenburg in eastern Germany, where they are cut off by advancing Soviet powers. The Germans power the detainees back to Stutthof. Walking in extreme winter conditions and treated fiercely by S.S. watches, thousands die during the walk. In late April 1945, the rest of the detainees are taken out from Stutthof via ocean, since Soviet powers surround Stutthof. Once more, several detainees are constrained into the ocean and shot. More than 25,000 detainees, one out of two, perish during the departure from Stutthof. Soviet powers entered Stutthof on May 9, 1945.

April 7, 1945

Death walk from Buchenwald death camp.

As the American powers approach, the Nazis start a mass clearing of detainees from the Buchenwald death camp and its subcamps. Right around 30,000 detainees are constrained on death walks from the advancing American powers. About 33% of these detainees die during the walks. On April 11, 1945, the enduring detainees assumed responsibility for the camp, right away before American powers enter around the same time.

April 26, 1945

Death walk from Dachau inhumane imprisonment.

Only three days before the Dachau camp's freedom, the S.S. powers send around 7,000 detainees on a death walk from Dachau south to Tegernsee. During the six-day death walk, any individual who cannot keep up or proceed was shot. Numerous others die of presentation, hunger, or sickness. American powers freed the Dachau camp on April 29, 1945. Toward the beginning of May 1945, American soldiers free the remaining detainees from the walk to Tegernsee.

Many individuals lost their positions as instructors, judges, cops—and scholastics at the nation's top colleges.

Throughout the following days, many German researchers and different erudite people would escape to the U.K., the U.S., and many different nations to secure their employment and lives. The Nazi system pushed out driving scientists, for example, Albert Einstein, Hans Krebs, and even public legend Fritz Haber, who had created substance weapons during World War I. The exceptional scholarly departure would have massive ramifications for Germany and the nations that took in the evacuees.

To catch a preview of the logical mass migration from 1930s Germany, we have followed 129 physicists' developments remembered for the 1936 List of Displaced German Scholars. The Notgemeinschaft Deutscher Wissenschaftler Ausland (Emergency Association of German Scholars in Exile), established by German neuropathologist and displaced person Philipp Schwartz in 1933, incorporated the report to help exiled scholastics find positions in other nations. The affiliation dispersed the rundown prudently to limit the danger of damage to the researchers in Germany. The rundown contains almost 1800 names in different fields. Many of the rundown individuals were Jewish, yet not all—some had Jewish life partners or other relatives, some upheld socialism, and others had stood in opposition to the legislature.

Every section closes with the position the individual held starting in 1936. Some blessed researchers were at that point safe with perpetual business abroad; others had the transient security of a position enduring a couple of months or a year. Nevertheless, a sizable segment of sections, especially for researchers from the get-go in their vocations, end with the contraction Unpl—unplaced.

The names in the material science area read like a who's who of mid-twentieth century material science: Hans Bethe, Felix Bloch, Max Born, Albert Einstein, James Franck, Otto Frisch, Fritz London, Lise Meitner, Erwin Schrödinger, Otto Stern, Leo Szilard, Edward Teller, Victor Weisskopf, Eugene Wigner.

Three of the uprooted researchers—Einstein, Franck, and Schrödinger—were at that point material science Nobel laureates; five more would eventually get the prize. A recent report found that 15% of physicists excused from German colleges represented 64% of all German material science references.

Luckily for those physicists and other uprooted researchers, associates from outside Germany acted rapidly to give help. The gathering's first president was physicist Ernest Rutherford. Finally, SPSL would help more than 2500 researchers from Germany and other occupied nations escape to the U.K. A close association in the U.S., the Emergency Committee in Aid of Displaced German (later Foreign) Scholars, protected more than 300 scholastics. The Notgemeinschaft kept point by point records of the researchers in danger and, working with associations like SPSL, helped secure positions abroad for many of them.

By far, most of the physicists on the rundown made due past World War II because of such endeavors. One particular striking case is Hans Hellmann, a spearheading quantum scientific expert who fled Nazi Germany just to be executed four years after the Soviet Union's Great Purge (see the going with article). All in all, uprooted German scholastics fared much better than other dislodged residents in Germany and occupied nations. "Would that shiploads of researchers, of specialists, or customary men, ladies, and youngsters have looked for and discovered the safe-haven that these people were assisted with discovering," Nathan Kravetz wrote in a foreword to 1993 reproducing of the dislodged researcher list.

During the mid-1930s, I.G. Farben turned into the single most significant contributor to the political race of Adolf Hitler. Even though it was marginally hesitant from the outset, since a portion of its key researchers were Jewish, in the conclusive year before Hitler won power, I.G. Farben gave 400,000 imprints to him and his Nazi gathering. It is sufficiently compensated. I.G. Farben, with Bayer, turned into the single biggest profiteer of German triumphs in World War II.

Hitler's accomplice:

In a letter to I.G. Farben chief Fritz der Meer in mid-1941, Dr. Otto Ambros applauded I.G. Farben's fellowship with the S.S. in speeding development of its Auschwitz-Buna plant and composed of a meal given by the camp administration where "all apportions worked for using the genuinely extraordinary administration of the inhumane imprisonment to the best bit of leeway of the Buna processing plant."

Even though Auschwitz was the biggest, most frightful site in history for killing people, its essential objective had been the formation of a monster I.G. Farben complex to deliver engineered petroleum and elastic as a feature of Germany's arrangements to conquer Europe and the world.

I.G. Farben was not just keen on fuel and elastic. Correspondence between Bayer supervisors and the Auschwitz authority included such trades as:

"We affirm your reaction, however, consider the cost of 200 RM [reichsmarks] per lady to be excessively high. We propose to pay close to 170 RM per lady. If this is worthy to you, the ladies will be set in our ownership. We need around 150 ladies,"

"We affirm your endorsement of the arrangement. If you do not mind plan for us 150 ladies in the ideal wellbeing,"

"Gotten the request for 150 ladies. Regardless of their macerated condition, they were viewed as agreeable. We will keep you educated regarding the improvements concerning the examinations,"

"The investigations were performed. All test people passed on. We will reach you in no time about another shipment."

I.G. Farben likewise had another use for Auschwitz. For those too old, too little, or too powerless to even consider working, it had Zyklon B, planned and created by an I.G. Farben auxiliary, Degesch.

At the point when their success plans crumbled and their massacre ended, the world expected that such men would rebuff. In August 1947, the U.S.-run Nuremberg War Criminal Tribunal against I.G. Farben started, with U.S. investigator Telford Taylor saying: *"These I.G. Farben hoodlums, not the maniac Nazi enthusiasts, are the fundamental war lawbreakers. On the off chance that the blame of these crooks is not exposed and on the off chance that they are not rebuffed, they will speak to a lot more noteworthy danger to the future tranquility of the world than Hitler on the off chance that he was as yet alive."*

However, the climate in Germany had changed; new enemies supplanted old ones. In July 1948, after almost a year, 10 of the 24 litigants were vindicated and 13, however, saw as liable on a portion of the charges of mass homicide, subjugation, and violations against humankind were condemned to gentle jail terms of one-and-a-half to eight years, including time previously served.

At the point when the war finished, the order economy was destroyed. Before the end of 1946, direct government distribution of assets—by decree, value controls, and apportioning plans—was disposed of. Duty rates were cut, too, even though they stayed high by contemporary principles. By any measure, the economy turned out to be less dependent upon government bearing. Regardless of expert financial specialists' negativity, assets that already would have been coordinated to create war merchandise immediately discovered their value to different employments. The business network did not share the financial analysts' misery. A survey of business heads in 1944 and 1945 found that only 8.5 percent of them thought the possibilities for their organization had declined in the after-war time frame. A contemporary writer noticed that in 1945-1946 organizations "had a huge and developing volume of unfilled requests for peacetime items." Truth be told, the end of wartime monetary controls matched with probably the most significant time of financial development in U.S. history. Since World War II, German psychotherapists are transparently and overwhelmingly analyzing their calling's past under the Nazi system.

However, some German state psychotherapists, who under the Nazi system a favored status, were obscure in that country up to that point.

A progression of articles in Psyche, the leading German psychoanalytic diary, has instigated a regularly malevolent and furious discussion among German psychoanalysts about this age from quite a while ago. As observed in general meetings with members just as with researchers and other people who survived the time, the issue is centered on the specialists who stayed in Germany during the war and turned into the calling's pioneers in the years that followed. Their participation with the Nazis, the pundits state, added up to the joint effort.

The discussion has an exceptional direness because the International Psychoanalytic Congress, the most significant gathering of the world's investigators, meets in Germany one year from now without precedent for a long time. Due to the short recollections of abuse and hostility to Semitism that period evoked for some psychoanalysts, the global gathering has up to this point declined to meet in Germany even though Germany's psychoanalytic affiliation is one of the world's biggest.

Numerous American psychoanalysts feel that it is fundamental that their German associates deal with the complicity of advisors in the Nazi period and face any sentiments of blame and disgrace that may wait. Such sentiments "make an obstruction that blocks an open, collegial connection among themselves and both their more youthful replacements and their Jewish associates," says Dr. Mortimer Ostow.

Adolf Hitler was simply debris among the rubble when World War II ended in Europe. The forlorn outcome was named "party time" by Germans — a more insightful term than they understood, for it likewise prepared to resurrection.

When the effectively evil-tempered Allies had conceded to the structure, timing, and marking subtleties of Germany's complete surrender, Berlin had been under the complete oversight of the Soviet Red Army for close to 7 days.

Adolf Hitler, unnerved of the possibility of being caught alive or being considered responsible for many killings, had married his accomplice Eva Braun and afterward, the two died by self-destruction of Berlin was chosen. Their cadavers were burned, and the cinders dissipated close to the purported Führerbunker, Hitler's headquarters later in the war. He did not need his cadaver to fall into the adversary's hands.

The Allies inevitably concurred that battle would authoritatively stop as of 11:01 p.m., Berlin time, on May 8, 1945. The oddly detailed planning was no mishap. It guaranteed that in Moscow, one hour in front of Berlin, the timekeepers would have ticked over to May 9, permitting the Soviets their day on which to review triumph in what was referred to in the USSR as the Great Patriotic War.

It was the Allied leaders who conveyed victorious addresses to their people. Winston Churchill remained on the top of the Health Ministry in London before cheering groups and broadcasted: *"This is your triumph! It is the triumph of the reason for an opportunity in each land. Throughout our entire history, we have never observed a more special day than this. Everybody has won."* The ousted previous and future French pioneer, Charles de Gaulle, also talked about triumph in his radiolocation, taking note that France's military order was available to mark the capitulation.

Then, the man who quickly succeeded Hitler that May, Admiral Karl Dönitz, gave a radio address lasting scarcely 30 seconds. He suggested his past transmission, on May 1, when he had declared Hitler's death and said his primary goal would be "to spare the lives of German individuals." To that end, he stated, he had requested that the military consent to unequivocal surrender.

"On May 8, at 23:01, the weapons will fall quiet," Dönitz said. His next significant public stage would be the Nuremberg Trials and his conviction for atrocities in 1946. He served only ten years in jail.

The prevailing worldwide view was and remained that the Germans' part in the war was that of the culprits, not the people in question after their nation set moving a worldwide war that proceeded to guarantee an expected 60 million lives and its powers eradicated 6 million Jews in the Holocaust.

On the ground — particularly after over a time of one end to the other purposeful publicity from the schoolyard up, twisting the picture of Hitler's Germany — this the truth was not as quickly self-evident.

Numerous German urban communities lay in rubble, either firebombed by western Allies (most prominently Dresden and Hamburg) or overwhelmed by the Soviets (Berlin). Invading officers are assessed to have assaulted more than 1 million German ladies. Racing into this no man's land was a mass migration of upwards of 14 million ethnic German exiles who either fled or were driven out of an area far toward the east of the present area.

Numerous youngsters were either dead, injured, caught, or damaged, regularly by atrocities they had perpetrated themselves or had found in the field. Then, the genuine degree of the Holocaust's shock, which did not highlight in Josef Goebbels' enemy of Semitic purposeful publicity, was becoming known. The prompt after war destruction became referred to casually as "Stunde Null": party time.

At first, Germany was isolated into four zones, one controlled by every one of the Allies to whom it had officially given up: the U.K., the U.S., the Soviet Union, and France. These partners of need had been apparent even before Germany's capitulation and had reemerged at the Potsdam meeting where the nation's definitive after war destiny was chosen.

In any case, in a stamped difference in technique after the correctional harmony terms following World War I, the Allies settled on a lighter touch, slowly guiding Germany once again into the global network. Reparations would even now be paid, however not at all to the degree of those mandated at Versailles in 1919.

The more extensive change from worldwide clash to the Cold War would before long prompt a more extended division of the nation — with the Soviet zone becoming East Germany, the GDR, and the other three zones becoming West Germany, or the Federal Republic.

Incomprehensibly, this new danger and division may have smoothed the rough way to the popular government for West Germany.

"I am very persuaded that the Cold War experience made it simpler, particularly for West German culture, to acknowledge being important for the Western world," Huber said. "It likewise made it simpler for them to embrace, deliberately, another majority rule constitution, which we have right up 'til the present time."

The Marshall Plan — an effective venture program started by the United States in 1948 to revamp Western Europe after the war and set it up for the long deadlock between private enterprise and Soviet socialism — added a budgetary motivation to invite another world request despite the recognizable danger from maybe Hitler's fiercest adversaries: Stalin and the USSR.

East and West:

West German international strategy quickly took a stab at outward compromise and reparation. Another and merely protective Bundeswehr was framed, and no unfamiliar military arrangements were affirmed until 1990. Right up 'til today, any missions abroad require consistently restored parliamentary endorsement.

At the point when Germany partakes in overseas activities, it is ordinarily offering strategic help for partners hitting the objectives, for example, in the alliance against the "Islamic State." It has also performed peacekeeping and protective tasks in an area that has been made sure about by NATO or other benevolent powers (with Afghanistan being the most significant model), West Germany, and later the reunified nation, driven the push for the formation of what is presently the European Union.

The legislature in Berlin likewise secured a verifiable duty regarding the Holocaust and the safeguard of Israel's presence as a feature of the country's raison d'etre.

Particularly in the early decades after the war, an apparition eclipsed such advances: the quantity of previous senior Nazis in places of influence in governments, courts, papers, and society.

"It required some investment for West Germany to make any genuine endeavor to confront the Nazi past," said Susan Neiman, a thinker and American Jew who has spent a lot of her vocation in Germany, writing a few books investigating the nation's relationship to the Holocaust, and is as of now with the Einstein Forum in Potsdam.

"It is regularly the situation that outsiders do not exactly acknowledge how evident this was, because the famous image of after war Germany was [Chancellor] Willy Brandt on his knees at the Warsaw Ghetto commemoration [in 1970]. That is the image we expected, and we needed to see. Most outsiders do not understand that numerous West Germans despised that offer of Brandt's. They thought it was not right; they assaulted Brandt for having left the nation during the war. The substantially more typical view in West Germany was not reparation or contrition for having been a culprit, however self-indulgence for having been a casualty."

Printed in the USA
CPSIA information can be obtained
at www.ICGtesting.com
CBHW070948310724
12433CB00017B/961

9 781917 394116